TWO BOOKS IN ONE

This new volume by Ruth Hatcher O'Mara is both a guide to teach you how to knit and a collection of patterns and instructions which will make it possible for even a beginner to create handsome garments for children wearing sizes 4 to 14. It is carefully planned to solve the problems every knitter encounters and packed with illustrations and diagrams to help answer your questions.

Also by Ruth Hatcher O'Mara

Easy Knitting for Babies and Toddlers

Published by Pocket Books Inc.

EASY KNITTING

CHILDREN'S SIZES 4 TO 14

RUTH HATCHER O'MARA

Illustrations by JUNE FERGUSON NICOLS

PUBLISHED BY POCKET BOOKS · NEW YORK

EASY KNITTING: CHILDREN'S SIZES 4 TO 14

Pocket Book edition published September, 1965
3rd printing............April, 1970

This original *Pocket Book* edition is printed from brand-new plates made from newly set, clear, easy-to-read type. *Pocket Book* editions are published by Pocket Books, a division of Simon & Schuster, Inc., 630 Fifth Avenue, New York, N.Y. 10020. Trademarks registered in the United States and other countries.

L

Standard Book Number: 671-75639-7.

Acknowledgments

The author expresses her gratitude to the following people, who have been so generous with their time and assistance in the preparation of this book:

John Bade, American Thread Company; Susan Bates, C. J. Bates & Co.; Ruth E. Fairbrother, Bear Brand—Fleisher Yarns; Carleen Goldsmith, Emile Bernat & Sons Co.; Patricia Quigley, Coats & Clark Inc.; Rosamay Winston, Columbia-Minerva Corp.; Mae E. MacLean, Reynolds Yarns Inc.; Alice Carroll, Spinnerin Yarn Co.; and Miriam Morrison Peake.

Foreword

This book is intended for skilled knitters as well as for beginners. It is based on the experience of my many years in the field of needlework, and is planned to solve the problems that knitters encounter, so that they may enjoy the pleasure and relaxation of knitting as much as I do.

All yarns recommended are readily available in one brand or another; on pages 206-210 you will find lists of many interchangeable yarns. Included is the brand name of the yarn used for each model pictured. Although no two manufacturers spin identical yarn, the interchangeable yarns listed are similar in weight and texture, and can be worked to the same gauge (I've tried them all myself).

In the "HOW-TO Section" you will find the meaning of all the abbreviations in French, German, Italian, and Spanish for the convenience of those who are more familiar with these languages. American needle sizes are given, but on page 201 you will find the comparable sizes of American and British knitting needles.

Now all you need is some yarn and a pair of needles to make some child happy and warm.

Contents

HOW-TO SECTION

Selecting the Proper Size

Sizes for this book are listed in age groups from 4 to 14, and chest measurements are given for each garment. However, children in the same age group are not all the same size. If possible, get the chest measurement of the child. Allowance should always be made for wearing sweaters over other clothing when taking body measurements. Select the size best suited to the child, regardless of age, according to the chest measurement.

Growing children with the same chest measurement may differ in height. You can change the length of back, front, and sleeves to underarms. If you are careful to follow the directions for GAUGE on page 173, your pieces, when blocked, will be sure to match the width measurements for the size you have selected. Although different models vary slightly in width, due to the styling, weight of yarn, or pattern, all are based on measurements from the Bureau of Standards.

Cable Trimmed Mohair Cardigan

shown on page 3
Sizes 4, 6, 8, 10, 12

Directions are for size 4. Changes for sizes 6, 8, 10, and 12 are in parentheses.
REYNOLDS "Mohair No. 1" was used for the original model. See chart on page 210 for comparable yarn.

MATERIALS: Mohair light weight—6 (7-8-9-9) ozs. 5 (5-7-7-7) buttons.
Knitting Needles: 1 pr of No. 8 or size required to knit to gauge. Dp needle for cables. No. 1 steel crochet hook.

GAUGE—The Most Important Word in Knitting
5 sts = 1"; 6 rows = 1".
Detailed drawings of how to make all of the basic stitches and all abbreviations used in these directions appear in the "How-To Section"—pages 169-210.

TEST PIECE: Cast on 20 sts. Work in pat for 24 rows. Piece should measure 4 × 4 inches. If too small, try larger-size needles; if too large, try smaller-size needles until correct gauge is obtained. While knitting, measure your work frequently to be sure you are maintaining the gauge.

MEASUREMENTS: At chest—buttoned—25 (27-29-31-33)"; across back at underarms—12½ (13½-14-15-16)"; across each front at underarms (borders not incl)—6 (7-7½-8-8½)"; sleeve width at upperarm—8¾ (9½-10-11-11½)"

(Continued on p. 4)

Cable Trimmed Mohair Cardigan instructions are on page 2.

PATTERN STITCH—Multiple of 3 sts plus 2.
Row 1—right side: P 2, * yarn in back, sl 1 as if to purl, p 2; repeat from * across. **Row 2:** K 2, * p 1, k 2; repeat from * across. Repeat these 2 rows for pat.

BACK: Cast on 62 (68-71-77-80) sts. Work even in pat until piece measures 10 (11-11½-12-12)" or desired length to underarms.
Raglan Armholes: Keeping continuity of pat, bind off 5 (6-6-7-7) sts at beg of next 2 rows. Dec 1 st each side every other row 15 (16-17-18-19) times. Bind off remaining 22 (24-25-27-28) sts.

LEFT FRONT: Cast on 31 (34-37-40-43) sts. **Row 1:** Work pat to last 8 sts, k 6, p 2 (front edge). **Row 2:** K 2, p 6, work pat to end of row. **Row 3:** Work pat to last 8 sts, slip next 3 sts to dp needle and hold in back of work, k next 3 sts, k 3 sts from dp needle (cable made), p 2. **Row 4:** Repeat row 2. **Rows 5-8:** Repeat rows 1 and 2 twice. Repeat these 8 rows until piece measures same as back to underarm. End at side edge.

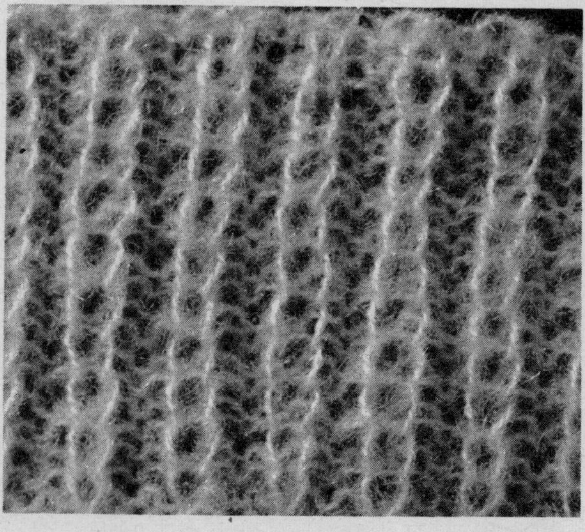

Raglan Armhole and Neck Shaping: Bind off 5 (6-6-7-7) sts at beg of next row. Dec 1 st at same edge every other row 10 (10-11-11-12) times—16 (18-20-22-24) sts. End at front edge. Bind off 6 (6-8-8-10) sts at beg of next row. Dec 1 st each side every other row 4 (5-5-6-6) times. Work last 2 sts tog.

RIGHT FRONT: Cast on 31 (34-37-40-43) sts. **Row 1:** P 2, k 6, work pat to end of row. **Row 2:** Work pat to last 8 sts, p 6, k 2. **Row 3:** P 2, cable over next 6 sts, complete row. Pat is now established, work to correspond to left front, reversing all shaping.

SLEEVES: Cast on 28 (28-34-34-34) sts. **Row 1:** Work pat across 11 (11-14-14-14) sts, k 6 for cable, work pat to end of row. **Row 2:** Work pat across 11 (11-14-14-14)sts, p 6, work pat to end. **Row 3:** Work across 11 (11-14-14-14) sts, cable over next 6 sts, complete row. Pat is now established. Working new sts in pat, inc 1 st each side every 1" 8 (10-8-10-12) times—44 (48-50-54-58) sts. Work even until sleeve measures 11 (11-11½-12½-13½)" or desired length to underarms.
Raglan Shaping: Bind off 5 (6-6-7-7) sts at beg of next 2 rows. Dec 1 st each side every other row 15 (16-17-18-19) times. Bind off remaining 4 (4-4-4-6) sts.

NECKBAND: Cast on 6 sts. Work in garter st (k every row) until band when stretched slightly fits around neck edge. Bind off.

BORDERS—Left Front: Cast on 6 sts. Work in garter st until piece when stretched slightly reaches from lower edge to top of neckband. Mark position of buttons along border sts, having first marker 1" from lower edge, top marker at center of neckband. Place remaining markers evenly between. **Right Front:** Work same as left front band, making buttonholes opposite markers. **Buttonholes:** Always starting at same edge, k 2, k 2 tog, yo, k 2. On next row work the yo as a st.

FINISHING: Steam-press pieces lightly. Sew sleeves to back and fronts. Sew neckband in place. Sew borders to front edges, having buttonhole band on right front. Sew underarm and sleeve seams. Work 1 row sc along each front edge and lower edge of cardigan. Work 1 row sc around sleeve edges.

Double Diamond Pullover

shown on page 7
Sizes 6, 8, 10, 12, 14

Directions are for size 6. Changes for sizes 8, 10, 12, and 14 are in parentheses.
COLUMBIA-MINERVA "Nantuk Knitting Worsted," was used for the Original Model.

MATERIALS: Nantuk Knitting Worsted—16 (18-20-22-24) ozs.
Knitting Needles: 1 pr each of No. 6 and No. 8 or size required to knit to gauge. 1 set of No. 6 dp needles.

GAUGE—The Most Important Word in Knitting
5 sts = 1"; 8 rows = 1".
Detailed drawing of how to make all of the basic stitches and all abbreviations used in these directions appear in the "How-To Section"—pages 169-210.

TEST PIECE: With No. 8 needles, cast on 15 sts. P 1 row, k 1 row for 16 rows. Piece should measure 3 × 2 inches. If too small, try larger-size needles; if too large, try smaller-size needles until correct gauge is obtained. Diamonds will tighten work a little but will block out. Measure width of piece occasionally to be sure you are not getting diamonds too tight. Use measurements given for width.

MEASUREMENTS: At chest—26 (28-30-32-35)"; across back and front at underarms—13 (14-15-16-17½)"; sleeve width at upperarm—10½ (11½-12-12½-13)".

PATTERN STITCH—Multiple of 12 sts plus 4.
Row 1—right side: P 7, * k 2 tog and before dropping sts from left hand needle, k again into first st—rc (right cross) made, p 10; repeat from *, ending rc, p 7.
Row 2: K 7, * yarn to front of work, sl 2 (always slip as to p with yarn in front), yarn in back, k 10; repeat from *, end sl 2, k 7.
(Continued on p. 8)

Double Diamond Pullover instructions are on page 6.

Row 3: P 6, * rc, skip next st, k into back loop of 2nd st, inserting needle through back loops of both sts, k tog the skipped st and 2nd st—lc (left cross) made, p 8; repeat from *, end rc, lc, p 6.
Row 4: K 6, * sl 1, k 2, sl 1, k 8; repeat from *, end last repeat k 6.
Row 5: P 5, * rc, p 2, lc, p 6; repeat from *, end rc, p 2, lc, p 5.
Row 6: K 5, * sl 1, k 4, sl 1, k 6; repeat from *, end last repeat k 5.
Row 7: P 4, * rc, p 4, lc, p 4; repeat from * across.
Row 8: K 4, * sl 1, k 6, sl 1, k 4; repeat from * across.
Row 9: P 3, * rc, p 6, lc, p 2; repeat from *, end last repeat p 3.
Row 10: K 3, * sl 1, k 8, sl 1, k 2; repeat from *, end last repeat k 3.
Row 11: P 2, * rc, p 8, lc; repeat from *, ending p 2.
Row 12: K 2, * sl 1, k 10, sl 1; repeat from *, ending k 2.
Row 13: P 2, k 1, * p 10, rc; repeat from *, end p 10, k 1, p 2.
Row 14: K 2, sl 1, * k 10, sl 2; repeat from *, end k 10, sl 1, k 2.
Row 15: P 2, * lc, p 8, rc; repeat from *, ending p 2.
Row 16: K 3, * sl 1, k 8, sl 1, k 2; repeat from *, end last repeat k 3.
Row 17: P 3, * lc, p 6, rc, p 2; repeat from *, end last repeat p 3.
Row 18: K 4, * sl 1, k 6, sl 1, k 4; repeat from *, end sl 1, k 4.
Row 19: P 4, * lc, p 4, rc, p 4; repeat from * across.
Row 20: K 5, * sl 1, k 4, sl 1, k 6; repeat from *, end last repeat k 5.
Row 21: P 5, * lc, p 2, rc, p 6; repeat from *, end last repeat p 5.
Row 22: K 6, * sl 1, k 2, sl 1, k 8; repeat from *, end last repeat k 6.
Row 23: P 6, * lc, rc, p 8; repeat from *, end last repeat p 6.
Row 24: K 7, * sl 2, k 10; repeat from *, end last repeat k 7.
Row 25: P 7, * rc, p 10; repeat from *, end last repeat p 7.
Row 26: Knit.
Rows 27–32: P 1 row, k 1 row 3 times.
Row 33: P 4, * rc, p 4; repeat from * across.
Row 34: K 4, * sl 2, k 4; repeat from * across.
Row 35: P 3, * rc, lc, p 2; repeat from *, end last repeat p 3.
Row 36: K 3, * sl 1, k 2; repeat from *, end last repeat k 3.
Row 37: P 2, * rc, p 2, lc; repeat from *, ending p 2.
Row 38: K 2, sl 1, * k 4, sl 2; repeat from *, end k 4, sl 1, k 2.
Row 39: P 2, k 1, * p 4, rc; repeat from *, ending p 4, k 1, p 2.
Row 40: K 2, sl 1, * k 4, sl 2; repeat from *, end k 4, sl 1, k 2.
Row 41: P 2, * lc, p 2, rc; repeat from *, ending p 2.
Row 42: K 3, * sl 1, k 2; repeat from *, ending sl 1, k 3.
Row 43: P 3, * lc, rc, p 2; repeat from *, end last repeat p 3.
Row 44: K 4, * sl 2, k 4; repeat from * across.

Row 45: P 4, * lc, p 4; repeat from * across.
Row 46: Knit.
Rows 47–52: P 1 row, k 1 row 3 times.
Repeat rows 1 through 52 for pattern.

BACK: With No. 6 needles, cast on 66 (70-76-80-88) sts. K 1, p 1 in ribbing for 2 (2-2½-2½-2½)". **Sizes 6, 8, and 12 only:** Slip a marker after the first (3rd-2nd) st from each end of needle. Carrying markers, work these sts in reverse stockinette st. They are not included in the pattern. **All sizes:** K 1 row. Change to No. 8 needles. Work even in pat until piece measures 10 (10½-11-12-12½)" or desired length to underarms.
Armholes: Keeping continuity of pat, bind off 2 (2-3-3-4) sts at beg of next 2 rows. Dec 1 st each side every other row 3 (3-4-4-4) times—56 (60-62-66-72) sts. Work even until armholes measure 5 (5½-6-6½-7¼)".
Shoulders: Bind off 6 (8-6-8-8) sts at beg of next 2 rows; 6 (6-7-7-8) sts at beg of next 4 rows. Slip remaining 20 (20-22-22-24) sts to a holder for back of neck.

(Continued on p. 10)

FRONT: Work same as back until armholes measure 3 (3½-4-4½-5)".

Neck and Shoulders: On next wrong side row, slip center 10 (10-12-12-14) sts to a holder. Working on sts of one side, at neck edge bind off 2 sts once. Dec 1 st at same edge every other row 3 times —18 (20-20-22-24) sts. Work even until armhole measures same as back. From arm edge bind off 6 (8-6-8-8) sts once; 6 (6-7-7-8) sts twice. Attach yarn at opposite neck edge and work other side to correspond.

SLEEVES: With No. 6 needles, cast on 36 (38-42-44-48) sts. K 1, p 1 in ribbing for 2 (2-2½-2½-3)". On last row inc 6 (6-4-4-6) sts evenly spaced—42 (44-46-48-54) sts. K 1 row slipping markers after first (2nd-3rd-4th-1st) st from each end of needle. Carry markers, working these sts in reverse stockinette st until more sts are added.

NOTE: To assure sleeve pat ending on same pat row as back at underarms, decide on sleeve length desired. Measure pattern on back from underarm to ribbing. Figure additional inches of sleeve desired less the ribbing worked. Pattern can be started on rows 1, 13, 27, 33, 39, and 47. Use back and front pieces as guide for row on which to start.

Work in pat for 1". Inc 1 st each side of next row and repeat incs every 1" 5 (5-6-6-5) times, working new sts in pat or keeping them in reverse stockinette st on outer side of markers as desired—54 (56-60-62-66) sts. Work even until sleeve measures 10 (11-12-13-15)" or desired length, end on same pat row as back and front.

Shaping: Bind off 2 (2-3-3-4) sts at beg of next 2 rows. Dec 1 st each side every other row until cap measures 2¾ (3-3¼-3½-3¾)". Bind off 2 sts at beg of next 6 rows. Bind off remaining sts.

FINISHING: Steam-press pieces to measurements. Sew shoulder, underarm, and sleeve seams. Sew in sleeves.

NECKBAND: With No. 6 dp needles, pick up 60 (64-68-72-76) sts all around neck edge including sts on holders. Work around and around in k 1, p 1 ribbing for 4 (4-5-5-6-6)". Bind off very loosely in ribbing.

Cowl-Neck Pullover

shown at right on page 13
Sizes 4, 6, 8, 10, 12

Directions are for size 4. Changes for sizes 6, 8, 10, and 12 are in parentheses.
BERNAT "Nylo Knitting Worsted" was used for the original model.

MATERIALS: Knitting Worsted—or—Nylon and Wool of Knitting Worsted weight—Main Color (MC) 8 (8-10-10-12) ozs; Contrasting Colors A and B—2 ozs of each color.
Knitting Needles: 1 pr each of No. 5 and No. 8 or size required to knit to gauge.

GAUGE—The Most Important Word in Knitting
5 sts = 1"; 7 rows = 1".
Detailed drawings of how to make all of the basic stitches and all abbreviations used in these directions appear in the "How-To Section"—pages 169-210.

TEST PIECE: With No. 8 needles, cast on 15 sts. Work in stockinette st (k 1 row, p 1 row) for 21 rows. Piece should measure 3 × 3 inches. If too small, try larger-size needles; if too large, try smaller-size needles until correct gauge is obtained. While knitting, measure your work frequently to be sure you are maintaining the gauge.

MEASUREMENTS: Chest—24 (26-28-30-32)"; across back or front at underarms—12 (13-14-15-16)"; sleeve width at upperarm—9 (10-10½-11-12)".

PATTERN STITCH—Multiple of 4 sts plus 3.
Row 1—right side: With MC, k 1, * yarn in front sl 1 as if to p, yarn in back, k 1; repeat from * across. **Row 2:** With MC, purl. **Row 3:** With A, sl 1, * k 1, yarn in front sl 1, yarn in back; re-
(Continued on p. 12)

peat from * across. **Row 4**: With A, purl. **Row 5**: With B, k 1, * yarn in back sl 1 as to p, k 3; repeat from *, ending sl 1, k 1. **Row 6**: With B, p 1, * with yarn in front sl 1, p 3; repeat from *, ending sl 1, p 1. **Rows 7 and 8**: With B, repeat rows 5 and 6. **Rows 9 and 10**: With A, k 1 row, p 1 row. Repeat these 10 rows for pat.

BACK: With MC and No. 5 needles, cast on 59 (63-67-71-75) sts. Work in stockinette st (k 1 row, p 1 row) for 6 rows. With A, k next 2 rows for hemline. Change to No. 8 needles. Starting with row 1, work even in pat for 24 rows, ending with pat row 4. Break off A and B. With MC, k next row inc 1 (2-3-4-5) sts evenly spaced—60 (65-70-75-80) sts. Continue in stockinette st with MC until piece measures 9 (10-11-11½-12)" or desired length to underarms. End with a p row.

Raglan Armholes and Neck Shaping: Bind off 2 (2-3-3-3) sts at beg of next 2 rows. **Dec Row**: K 2, k 2 tog, k to last 4 sts, sl 1, k 1, psso, k 2. P 1 row. Repeat these 2 rows 9 (11-12-14-16) times more—36 (37-38-39-40) sts, end with a k row. On next row p 12; slip remaining sts to a holder. Working on sts of one side at neck edge bind off 2 sts twice, dec 1 st at same edge every other row once and at arm edge continue raglan decs 5 times more. K last 2 sts tog. Slip center 12 (13-14-15-16) sts to a holder, attach yarn and complete other side to correspond, reversing shaping.

FRONT: Work same as back.

SLEEVES: With MC and No. 5 needles, cast on 36 (38-38-40-42) sts. K 1, p 1 in ribbing for 2". Change to No. 8 needles. Work in stockinette st, inc 1 st each side every 8th row 5 (6-7-8-9) times—
(Continued on p. 14)

Cowl-Neck Pullover instructions are on page 11.
Lightweight Pullover instructions are on page 14.

46 (50-52-56-60) sts. Work even until sleeve measures 10½ (11½-12½-13½-15)" or desired length to underarm.
Raglan Shaping: Bind off 3 sts at beg of next 2 rows. Work decs same as for back until 10 sts remain. Bind off.

COLLAR—Make 2 Pieces: With No. 5 needles and MC, cast on 55 (59-63-67-75) sts. Work in stockinette st for ¾". End with a p row. Change to No. 8 needles, attach A and k 2 rows for hemline. Work even in pat for 24 rows, ending with row 4. On last row dec 1 st at end of row. Change to No. 5 needles. With MC, k 1, p 1 in ribbing for 2½ (2½-3-3-3)". Bind off in ribbing.

FINISHING: Steam-press pieces lightly. Sew sleeves to front and back. Sew underarm and sleeve seams. Sew ends of collar tog, matching pat. Sew collar to neck edge with seams at shoulders. Hem collar and lower edge.

Lightweight Pullover

shown at left on page 13
Sizes 4, 6, 8, 10, 12, 14

Directions are for size 4. Changes for sizes 6, 8, 10, 12, and 14 are in parentheses.
BERNAT "Nylo Sports Yarn" was used for the original model.

MATERIALS: Nylon and Wool Sport Yarn—or—Sayelle Nantuk of Sports Yarn weight—Main Color (MC)—9 (10-11-12-13-14) ozs; Contrasting Colors A and B—1 (1-2-2-2-2) ozs of each color.
Knitting Needles: 1 pr each of No. 3 and No. 5 or size required to knit to gauge. 1 set of No. 3 dp needles.

GAUGE—The Most Important Word in Knitting
6 sts = 1"; 8 rows = 1".
Detailed drawings of how to make all of the basic stitches and all abbreviations used in these directions appear in the "How-To Section"—pages 169-210.

TEST PIECE: With No. 5 needles and MC, cast on 20 sts. Work even in pat for 24 rows. Piece should measure 3⅓ × 3 inches. If too small, try larger-size needles; if too large, try smaller-size needles until correct gauge is obtained. While knitting, measure your work frequently to be sure you are maintaining the gauge.

MEASUREMENTS: Chest—24 (26-28-30-32-34)"; across back or front at underarms—12 (13-14-15-16-17)"; sleeve width at upper-arm—9½ (10-11-11½-12½-13)".

PATTERN STITCH—Multiple of 6 sts plus 2.
Row 1: Skip first st, k the next st and leave on needle, k the skipped st, slip both sts from left-hand needle (right twist st made); * p 4, make twist st over next 2 sts; repeat from * across. **Row 2**: P 2, * k 4, p 2; repeat from * across. **Row 3**: Insert point of right hand needle from back to front between next 2 sts, k the next st (2nd st) through front loop of st and leave on left hand needle, k the skipped st (left twist st made); * p 4, make left twist st over next 2 sts; repeat from * across. **Row 4**: P 2, * k 4, p 2; repeat from * across. Repeat these 4 rows for pat.

BACK: With No. 3 needles and MC, cast on 72 (78-84-90-96-102) sts. K 1, p 1 in ribbing for 1 (1-1½-1½-1½-1½)". Attach A, p 1 row then work in ribbing for 5 rows. Break off A. Attach B, p 1 row then work 5 rows of ribbing. Break off B. Attach MC, p 1 row. **Pat—Row 1—right side**: P 5 sts, slip a marker on needle, work row 1 of pat across next 62 (68-74-80-86-92) sts, slip another marker on needle, p 5. **Row 2**: K 5, slip marker, work row 2 of pat across to next marker, slip marker, k 5. Keeping 5 sts each side in reverse stockinette st, work even until piece measures 9 (10-11-11½-12-12)" or desired length to underarms.
Armholes: Keeping continuity of pat, bind off 3 (4-4-5-6-6) sts at beg of next 2 rows. Dec 1 st each side every other row 3 (3-3-4-4-5) times—60 (64-70-72-76-80) sts. Work even until armholes measure 5 (5¼-5½-6-6½-7)".
Shoulders: Bind off 6 (7-8-8-8-8) sts at beg of next 4 rows; 7 (7-7-8-8-9) sts at beg of next 2 rows. Slip remaining 22 (22-24-24-28-30) sts to a holder for back of neck.

(Continued on p. 16)

FRONT: Work same as back until piece measures 1" less than back to underarms. End with pat row 2 or 4.

Neck and Armholes: Work across 36 (39-42-45-48-51) sts, slip remaining sts to a holder. Working on sts of one side, at neck edge dec 1 st every other row 3 times; every 4th row 8 (8-9-9-11-12) times; *meanwhile*—when underarm edge measures same as back, from arm edge bind off 3 (4-4-5-6-6) sts once. Dec 1 st at same edge every other row 3 (3-3-4-4-5) times—19 (21-23-24-24-25) sts remain after all decs. When armhole measures same as back from arm edge bind off 6 (7-8-8-8-8) sts twice; 7 (7-7-8-8-9) sts once. Attach yarn at neck edge, work other side to correspond.

SLEEVES: With No. 3 needles and MC, cast on 40 (42-44-46-48-52) sts. K 1, p 1 in ribbing for 2". With A, p 1 row then work 5 rows of ribbing. Break off A. With B, p 1 row then work 5 rows of ribbing. Break off B. With MC, p 1 row inc 4 (2-6-4-8-10) sts evenly spaced—44 (44-50-50-56-62) sts. Change to No. 8 needles.

Pat—Row 1: Work row 1 of pat across all sts and continue in pat, inc 1 st each side every 6th row 7 (8-8-9-10-9) times—58 (60-66-68-76-80) sts. Work even until sleeve measures 10½ (11-11½-12½-13½-15)" or desired length.

Shaping: Bind off 3 (4-4-5-6-6) sts at beg of next 2 rows. Dec 1 st each side every other row until cap measures 3 (3¼-3½-3¾-4-4¼)" Bind off 3 sts at beg of next 6 rows. Bind off remaining sts.

FINISHING: Steam-press pieces lightly. Sew shoulder, underarm and sleeve seams. Sew in sleeves.

Neckband: With right side to you, using No. 3 dp needles and MC, k 22 (22-24-24-28-30) sts across back of neck from holder; pick up 42 (46-48-50-52-54) sts along left side of neck, pick up 1 st in center, slip a marker each side of this center st; pick up 41 (45-47-49-51-53) sts along right neck edge—106 (114-120-124-132-138) sts. Break off MC. With A, k 1 rnd. **Rnd 2:** Work in k 1, p 1 ribbing, dec 1 st each side of center st—always k center st. **Rnd 3:** With A, work even in ribbing. **Rnd 4:** With A, work in ribbing, dec 1 st each side of center st. Break off A. **Rnd 5:** With B, k 1 rnd. **Rnd 6:** With B, work in ribbing, dec 1 st each side of center st. Work 1 rnd even. **Rnd 8:** Dec 1 st each side of center st. Bind off in ribbing, working 2 sts tog each side of center st. Finish off all ends neatly. Steam-press neckband lightly.

Bulky Raglan Jacket

shown on page 19
Sizes 4, 6, 8, 10, 12, 14

Directions are for size 4. Changes for sizes 6, 8, 10, 12, and 14 are in parentheses.
AMERICAN THREAD COMPANY "Dawn Knitting Worsted" was used for the original model.

MATERIALS: Knitting Worsted—or—Orlon yarn of Knitting Worsted weight—12 (14-14-16-18-19) ozs. Zipper for closing.
Knitting Needles: 1 pr each of No. 7 and No. 11 or size required to knit to gauge. Size F crochet hook.

GAUGE—The Most Important Word in Knitting
4 sts = 1″; 6 rows = 1″.
Detailed drawings of how to make all of the basic stitches and all abbreviations used in these directions appear in the "How-To Section"—pages 169-210.

TEST PIECE: With No. 11 needles, cast on 12 sts. Work in pat for 18 rows. Piece should measure 3 × 3 inches. If too small, try larger-size needles; if too large, try smaller-size needles until correct gauge is obtained. While knitting, measure your work frequently to be sure you are maintaining the gauge.

MEASUREMENTS: At chest closed—25 (27-29-31-33-35)″; across back at underarms—12 (13-14-15-16-17)″; across each front at underarms—6¼ (6¾-7¼-7¾-8¼-8¾)″; sleeve width at upperarm—9¾ (10¼-11¼-11¾-12¾-13¼)″.

RIBBING—Row 1: P 1, * k 1, p 1; repeat from * across. **Row 2:** K 1, * p 1, k 1; repeat from * across. Repeat these 2 rows for ribbing.

PATTERN STITCH—Uneven multiple of sts.
Row 1—right side: K 1, * with yarn in back, sl 1 as to purl, k 1; repeat from * across. **Row 2:** Purl. Repeat these 2 rows for pattern.
(Continued on p. 18)

BACK: With No. 7 needles, cast on 49 (53-57-61-65-69) sts. Work in ribbing for 2". End with row 2. Change to No. 11 needles. Work even in pat until piece measures 8½ (9-10-11-11½-12)" or desired length to underarms. Mark each end of last row for armholes.

Raglan Armholes: Keeping continuity of pat, dec 1 st each side every other row 16 (18-19-21-22-24) times. Loosely bind off remaining 17 (17-19-19-21-21) sts for back of neck.

RIGHT FRONT: With No. 7 needles, cast on 25 (27-29-31-33-35) sts. Work in ribbing for 2". Change to No. 11 needles. Work even in pat until same length as back to underarm. End at front edge with row 2 of pat. Mark beg of last row at underarm.

Raglan Armhole and Neck Shaping: Dec 1 st at arm edge every other row twice. End with a p row. Continuing arm edge decs every other row 14 (16-17-19-20-22) times more, at front edge dec 1 st every 4th row 7 (7-8-8-9-9) times. K last 2 sts tog.

LEFT FRONT: Work to correspond to right front, reversing all shaping. Front edge will be at end of pat row 1.

SLEEVES: With No. 7 needles, cast on 27 (29-31-33-35-37) sts. Work in ribbing for 2". On last row inc 1 st each side—29 (31-33-35-37-39) sts. Work in pat, inc 1 st each side every 1¼" 5 (6-6-7-7-8) times—39 (43-45-49-51-55) sts. Work even until sleeve measures 11 (12-13-14-15-15)" or desired length to underarm. Mark each end of last row.

Raglan Shaping: Dec 1 st each side every other row until 7 sts remain. On next row bind off working 2 sts tog at each end.

COLLAR: With No. 7 needles, cast on 87 (89-91-93-95-97) sts. Work in ribbing for 2". Keeping continuity of ribbing, bind off 3 sts at beg of every row until collar measures 3 (3-3½-3½-3½-3½)" measured through center back. Bind off remaining sts.

FINISHING: Steam-press pieces lightly. Sew sleeves to fronts and back from marked rows to neck edge. Sew underarm and sleeve seams. With right side to you, work 1 row sc along each front edge from first row of neck decs to lower edge. Sew shaped edge of collar to neck edge starting and ending at sc row. Sew in zipper.

Bulky Raglan Jacket instructions are on page 17.

Lightweight Cardigan and Slipon

shown on page 21
Sizes 6, 8, 10, 12

Directions are for size 6. Changes for sizes 8, 10, and 12 are in parentheses.
COLUMBIA-MINERVA "3 Ply Fingering Yarn" was used for the original models.

MATERIALS: 3 Ply Fingering Yarn. **Cardigan**—Main Color (MC) —6 (7-7-8) ozs; Colors A and B—1 (1-2-2) ozs of each color.
Slipon—Main Color—3 (4-5-6) ozs; Colors A and B—1 oz of each color. 5 buttons for Cardigan.
Knitting Needles: 1 pr each of No. 2 and No. 3 or size required to knit to gauge.

GAUGE—The Most Important Word in Knitting
Pattern st on No. 3 needles—8 sts = 1"; 13 rows = 1".
Ribbing on No. 3 needles—8 sts = 1"; 12 rows = 1".
Detailed drawings of how to make all of the basic stitches and all abbreviations used in these directions appear in the "How-To Section"—pages 169-210.

TEST PIECE: With No. 3 needles, cast on 23 sts. Work in pat for 26 rows. Piece should measure 3 × 2 inches. If too small, try larger-size needles; if too large, try smaller-size needles until correct gauge is obtained. While knitting, measure your work frequently to be sure you are maintaining the gauge.

MEASUREMENTS: **Cardigan**—at chest buttoned—27 (29½-31½-33)"; across back at underarms—13 (14-15-16)"; across each front, not incl border—6¾ (7¼-7¾-8¼); sleeve width at upperarm—10½ (11-11½-12)".

(Continued on p. 22)

Lightweight Cardigan and Slipon instructions are on page 20.

PATTERN STITCH—Multiple of 4 sts plus 3.
Row 1—right side: With A, k 3, * with yarn in back, sl 1, k 3; repeat from * across. **Row 2:** With A, purl. **Row 3:** With B, k 1, * yarn in back sl 1, k 3; repeat from *, ending sl 1, k 1. **Row 4:** With B, purl. **Rows 5 and 6:** Repeat rows 1 and 2. **Rows 7 and 8:** With MC, repeat rows 3 and 4. Repeat these 8 rows for pat.

RIBBING—Row 1: K 1, * p 1, k 1; repeat from * across. **Row 2:** P 1, * k 1, p 1; repeat from * across. Repeat these 2 rows for all ribbing.

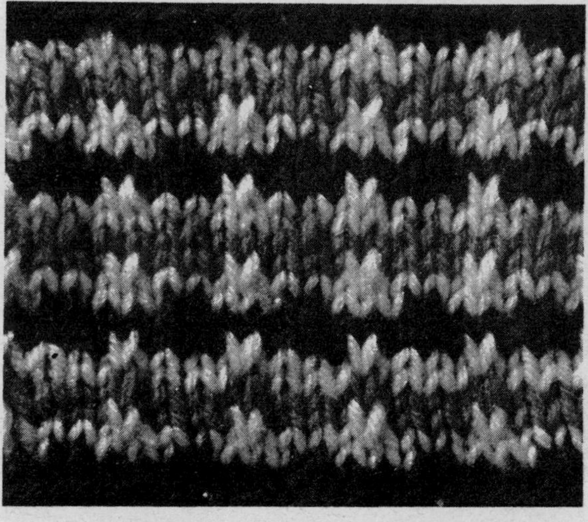

CARDIGAN

BACK: With No. 2 needles and MC, cast on 103 (111-119-127) sts. Work in ribbing for 2 (2-2½-2½)". End with row 1. Purl 1 row. Change to No. 3 needles and continue in ribbing until piece measures 11½ (12-12½-12½)" or desired length to underarms.
Raglan Armholes: Bind off 2 sts at beg of next 2 rows. Keeping continuity of ribbing, dec 1 st each side every other row until 31 (35-37-39) sts remain. Bind off.

RIGHT FRONT: With No. 2 needles and MC, cast on 61 (65-69-73) sts. Work ribbing same as back. End with row 1 at side edge. **Next Row:** Inc 1 st in first st, p to last 11 sts and slip them to a holder for border sts. Change to No. 3 needles. Attach A, work row 1 of pat across 51 (55-59-63) sts and continue until same length as back to underarm, ending at side edge.
Raglan Armhole and Neck Shaping: Bind off 2 sts at beg of row, work to last 2 sts, k 2 tog. Keeping continuity of pat, shape both sides at same time. **Neck Edge**—Dec 1 st every 6th row 5 (6-6-7) times, then every 4th row 4 (5-6-7) times—meanwhile at **Arm Edge** dec 1 st every other row until 2 sts remain. K 2 tog.
Slip 11 border sts to No. 2 needle and continue in ribbing until band, when stretched slightly, reaches to shoulder, work about 3" more. Slip sts to a holder. Mark position of 5 buttons along border sts, having first marker in center of lower ribbing and top marker at beg of neck shaping. Space 3 others evenly between.

LEFT FRONT: Work to correspond to right front, reversing all shaping and making buttonholes opposite markers. **Buttonholes:** Starting at front edge, rib 4 sts, bind off next 3 sts, complete row. On next row cast on 3 sts over the bound-off sts. End last row of ribbing at front edge. **Next Row:** Starting at front edge, rib 11 sts and slip them to a holder, purl remaining sts, inc 1 st in last st. Change to No. 3 needles. Work row 1 of pat and complete as right front.

SLEEVES: With No. 2 needles and MC, cast on 53 (57-61-67) sts. Work in ribbing for 2½". End with row 1. Purl 1 row. Change to No. 3 needles and continue ribbing, inc 1 st each side every 6th row 16 (16-17-17) times—85 (89-95-101) sts. Work even until sleeves measure 13 (14-15-16)" or desired length.
Raglan Shaping: Bind off 2 sts at beg of next 2 rows. Dec 1 st each side every other row until 13 sts remain. Bind off.

FINISHING: Steam-press pieces lightly. Sew sleeves to fronts and back. Sew underarm and sleeve seams. Sew bands to fronts and top of sleeves. Adjust band to meet at center back of neck, weave ends tog and sew to neck edge. Sew on buttons.

(Continued on p. 24)

SLIPON

BACK: With No. 2 needles and MC, cast on 103 (111-119-127) sts. Work in ribbing for 2 (2-2½-2½)". End with row 1. Purl 1 row. Change to No. 3 needles and work even in pat until piece measures 9 (10-11-11½)" or desired length to underarms.

Armholes: Bind off 7 (8-8-9) sts at beg of next 2 rows. Dec 1 st each side every other row 3 times—83 (89-97-103) sts. Work even until armholes measure 5¾ (6¼-6¾-7¼)".

Shoulders: Bind off 8 (9-10-11) sts at beg of next 6 rows—35 (35-37-37) sts. Change to No. 2 needles. Work in ribbing for 1". Bind off loosely in ribbing.

FRONT: Work same as back until 1 pat row less than back at underarms, ending with a row on right side. **Next Row**: P 51 (55-59-63) sts, slip these sts to holder, bind off 1 st, complete row.

Armhole and Neck Shaping: At arm edge bind off 7 (8-8-9) sts once, dec 1 st at same edge every other row 3 times and at neck edge, dec 1 st every 4th row 17 (17-18-18) times—24 (27-30-33) sts. Work even until armhole measures same as back.

Shoulder: From arm edge bind off 8 (9-10-11) sts 3 times. Attach yarn at center front and work other side to correspond, reversing all shaping.

NECKBAND: With right side to you, using No. 2 needles and MC, pick up 60 (64-68-72) sts along left neck edge, pick up 1 st at center and mark this st, pick up 60 (64-68-72) sts along right neck edge—121 (129-137-145) sts. Work 1 row of ribbing. Keeping continuity of ribbing, dec 1 st each side of center st every other row until band measures same as back neckband. Bind off loosely in ribbing. Sew shoulder and neckband seams tog.

ARMBANDS: With right side to you, using No. 2 needles and MC, pick up 113 (125-129-137) sts along armhole edge. Work in ribbing for 1". Bind off loosely in ribbing.

FINISHING: Sew underarm seams. Steam-press lightly.

Ribbed Jacket

shown on page 27
Sizes 8, 10, 12, 14

Directions are for size 8. Changes for sizes 10, 12, and 14 are in parentheses.
COLUMBIA-MINERVA "Calibar" was used for the original model.

MATERIALS: Bulky Quick Knit Yarn—12 (14-16-18) ozs. 5 (5-6-6) buttons.
Knitting Needles: 1 pr each of No. 6 and 10½ or size required to knit to gauge.

GAUGE—The Most Important Word in Knitting
7 sts = 2"; 9 rows = 2".
Detailed drawings of how to make all of the basic stitches and all abbreviations used in these directions appear in the "How-To Section"—pages 169-210.

TEST PIECE: With No. 10½ needles, cast on 15 sts. Work in rib pat for 9 rows. Piece should measure 4 × 2 inches. If too small, try larger-size needles; if too large, try smaller-size needles until correct gauge is obtained. While knitting, measure your work frequently to be sure you are maintaining the gauge.

MEASUREMENTS: At chest, buttoned—29 (31-33-35)"; across back at underarms—14 (15-16-17)"; across each front at underarms—7¾ (8½-9-9½)"; sleeve width at upperarm—10½ (11½-12-12½)".

PATTERN STITCH—Uneven multiple of stitches.
Row 1—wrong side: K 1, * p 1, k 1; repeat from * across. **Row 2:** P 1, * k 1, p 1; repeat from * across. Repeat these 2 rows.
(Continued on p. 26)

BACK: With No. 6 needles, cast on 41 (45-47-51) sts. Work in pat for 7 rows, ending with row 1. **Inc. Row:** Rib 7 (11-7-9) sts, k, p and k in next st (2 sts inc), * rib 7, inc 2 sts in next st; repeat from * 2 (2-3-3) times more, rib last 9 (9-7-9) sts—49 (53-57-61) sts. Continue in rib pat until piece measures 7 (8-8½-8½)" or desired length to underarms. Mark each end of last row.

Armholes: Keeping continuity of ribbing, dec 1 st each side every row 5 (6-6-7) times—39 (41-45-47) sts. Work even until armholes measure 6 (6-7-7½)" above marked row.

Shoulders: Bind off 12 (13-14-15) sts at beg of next 2 rows. Bind off remaining 15 (15-17-17) sts for back of neck.

LEFT FRONT: With No. 6 needles, cast on 27 (29-31-33) sts. Work in rib pat for 7 rows. Change to No. 10½ needles and continue until same length as back to underarms. End with row 1 at side edge. Mark end of last row.

Armhole: Dec 1 st at arm edge every row 6 times—21 (23-25-27) sts. Work even until 4 (4½-5-5½)" above marked row. End at front edge.

Neck and Shoulder: Bind off 6 (7-8-9) sts at beg of next row. Dec 1 st at same edge every row 3 times—12 (13-14-15) sts. Work even until armhole measures same as back. From arm edge bind off all sts.

Mark position of 5 (5-6-6) buttons evenly spaced along front edge, having first marker 1" from lower edge, top marker 2 rows below neck bind off, space others evenly between.

(Continued on p. 28)

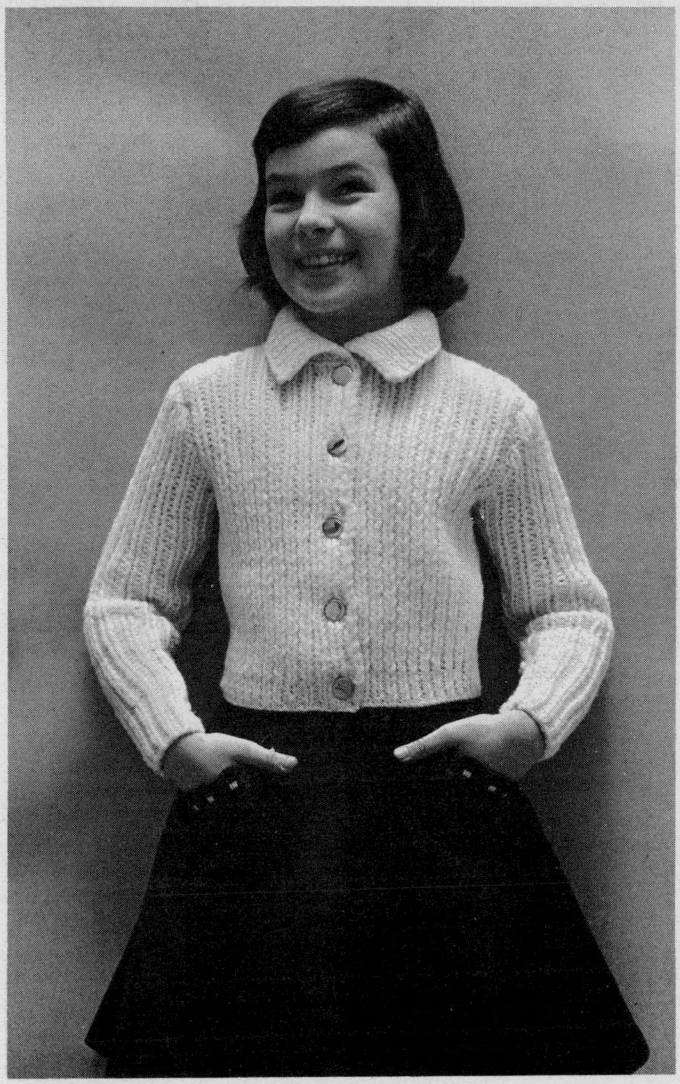

Ribbed Jacket instructions are on page 25.

RIGHT FRONT: Work to correspond to left front, reversing all shaping and making buttonholes opposite markers. **Buttonholes:** Starting at front edge (beg of row 2), p 1, k 1, p 2 tog, yo, complete row. On next row work the yo as a st.

SLEEVES: With No. 6 needles, cast on 23 (23-25-25) sts. Work in pat for 2½ (2½-3-3)". End with row 1. Change to No. 10½ needles. Inc 1 st each side of next row and repeat incs every 1½" 6 (7-7-8) times more—37 (39-41-43) sts. Work even until sleeve measures 13 (14-15-16)" or desired length to underarms. Mark each end of last row.
Shaping: Dec 1 st each side every other row 6 (7-7-8) times. Work even for 2 (4-6-6) rows. Bind off in ribbing.

COLLAR: With No. 6 needles, cast on 71 (73-77-79) sts. Work in rib pat for 3". Bind off loosely in ribbing.

FINISHING: Steam-press pieces lightly, stretching ribbing to measurements. Sew shoulder seams. Sew sleeves to armholes between marked rows. Sew underarm and sleeve seams. Sew cast-on edge of collar to neck edge. Face fronts with ribbon if desired. Slit ribbon under buttonholes and whip ribbon to buttonholes. Sew tape across neck edge on wrong side. Sew on buttons.

Cabled Cardigan

shown at right on page 31
Sizes 4, 6, 8, 10, 12, 14

Directions are for size 4. Changes for sizes 6, 8, 10, 12, and 14 are in parentheses.
AMERICAN THREAD COMPANY "Dawn Knitting Worsted" was used for the original model.

MATERIALS: Knitting Worsted: 12 (14-16-18-20-20) ozs. 7 buttons.
Knitting Needles: 1 pr each of No. 5 and No. 7 or size required to knit to gauge. 1 dp needle for cabling.

GAUGE—The Most Important Word in Knitting

6 sts = 1"; 8 rows = 1".

Detailed drawings of how to make all of the basic stitches and all abbreviations used in these directions appear in the "How-To Section"—pages 169-210.

TEST PIECE: With No. 7 needles, cast on 30 sts. Work in pat for 21 rows. Piece should measure 5 × 3 inches. If too small, try larger-size needles; if too large, try smaller-size needles until correct gauge is obtained. While knitting, measure your work frequently to be sure you are maintaining the gauge.

MEASUREMENTS: At chest, buttoned—25¼ (27¼-29½-31¼-33-35)"; across back at underarms—12¼ (13¼-14½-15¼-16-17)"; across each front, border sts incl—7 (7½-8¼-8½-9-9½)"; sleeve width at upper-arm—9½ (10-11-11½-12-12½)".

PATTERN STITCH—Row 1—right side: P 1 (4-1-3-5-1), * k 2, p 3, k 6, p 3; repeat from *, ending k 2, p 1 (4-1-3-5-1). **Row 2 and all even rows:** Purl. **Rows 3, 4, 5, and 6:** Repeat Rows 1 and 2 twice. **Row 7:** P 1 (4-1-3-5-1), * k 2, p 3, slip next 3 sts to dp needle and hold in front of work, k next 3 sts, k 3 sts from dp needle (cable made), p 3; repeat from * across, ending k 2, p 1 (4-1-3-5-1). **Row 8:** Purl. Repeat these 8 rows for pat.

BACK: With No. 5 needles, cast on 74 (80-88-92-96-102) sts. K 1, p 1 in ribbing for 2 (2-2-2½-2½-2½)". Change to No. 7 needles. Work even in pat until piece measures 9 (10-10½-11-12-12½)" or desired length to underarms.

Armholes: Bind off 3 (3-4-4-4-4) sts at beg of next 2 rows. Keeping continuity of pat and discontinuing cables when not enough sts, dec 1 st each side every other row 3 (4-4-4-4-5) times—62 (66-72-76-80-84) sts. Work even until armholes measure 4¾ (5-5½-6-6½-7)".

Shoulders: Bind off 5 (5-6-6-6-7) sts at beg of next 4 rows; 5 (6-6-7-7-7) sts at beg of next 4 rows. Bind off remaining 22 (22-24-24-28-28) sts for back of neck.

LEFT FRONT: With No. 5 needles, cast on 42 (46-50-52-54-56) sts. K 1, p 1 in ribbing until same length as back, inc 2 (1-1-1-1-2) sts

(Continued on p. 30)

on last row—44 (47-51-53-55-58) sts. Change to No. 7 needles. **Pat Row 1:** Starting at side edge work pat across to last 7 sts, ending last repeat k 3 (3-1-1-1-3), rib last 7 sts (front border). **Row 2:** Rib 7, p to end of row. Keeping continuity of pat as established and 7 rib sts at front edge, work even until same length as back to underarm. End at side edge.

Armhole: Bind off 3 (3-4-4-4-4) sts at beg of next row. Dec 1 st at same edge every other row 3 (4-4-4-4-5) times—38 (40-43-45-47-49) sts. Work even until armhole measures 2¾ (3-3½-4-4½-5)". End at front edge.

Neck and Shoulder: At beg of next row work 10 sts and slip them to a holder. At neck edge bind off 2 (2-2-2-3-3) sts every other row twice. Dec 1 st at same edge every other row 4 (4-5-5-5-5)

(Continued on p. 32)

Cabled Cardigan instructions are on page 28.
Olympic V Neck Pullover instructions are on page 33.

times—20 (22-24-26-26-28) sts. When armhole measures same as back from arm edge bind off 5 (5-6-6-6-7) sts twice; 5 (6-6-7-7-7) sts twice.

Mark position of 6 buttons evenly spaced on border sts, having first marker 1" from lower edge; space 5 others evenly, allowing for 7th button in neckband.

RIGHT FRONT: Work ribbing as left front, making first buttonhole opposite marker. **Buttonhole:** Starting at front edge, rib 3, bind off next 2 sts, complete row. On next row cast on 2 sts over the bound-off sts. End ribbing at front edge. **Pat Row 1—Sizes 4-6-14:** Rib 7, k 3, * p 3, k 2, p 3, k 6; repeat from *, ending p 3, k 2, p 1 (4-1). **Sizes 8-10-12:** Rib 7, k 1, * p 3, k 6, p 3, k 2; repeat across, ending p 1 (3-5). Pat is now established, complete to correspond to left front, repeating buttonholes opposite markers.

SLEEVES: With No. 5 needles, cast on 40 (42-46-48-52-52) sts. K 1, p 1 in ribbing for 2 (2-2½-2½-2½-3)". On last row inc 4 (2-4-2-4-4) sts—44 (44-50-50-56-56) sts. Change to No. 7 needles. **Pat Row 1—Sizes 4 and 6:** K 2, * p 3, k 6, p 3, k 2; repeat from *, ending p 3, k 6, p 3, k 2. **Sizes 8 and 10:** * P 3, k 2, p 3, k 6; repeat from *, ending p 3, k 2, p 3. **Sizes 12 and 14:** K 3, * p 3, k 2, p 3, k 6; repeat from *, ending p 3, k 2, p 3, k 3. Keeping continuity of pat and working new sts in pat as added, inc 1 st each side every 8th row 6 (8-8-9-8-9) times—56 (60-66-68-72-74) sts. Work even until sleeve measures 10 (11-11½-12-13-15)" or desired length.

Shaping: Bind off 3 (3-4-4-4-4) sts at beg of next 2 rows. Dec 1 st each side every other row until 30 (30-30-32-32-32) sts remain. Bind off 3 sts at beg of next 4 rows. Bind off remaining sts.

FINISHING: Steam-press pieces lightly. Sew shoulder, underarm, and sleeve seams. Sew in sleeves.

NECKBAND: With right side to you, using No. 5 needles pick up 58 (60-64-68-72-76) sts all around neck edge including sts on holders. K 1, p 1 in ribbing, working last buttonhole when band measures ½". Work ½" more. Bind off loosely in ribbing. Sew on buttons.

Olympic V Neck Pullover

shown at left on page 31
Sizes 6, 8, 10, 12, 14

Directions are for size 6. Changes for sizes 8, 10, 12, and 14 are in parentheses.
AMERICAN THREAD COMPANY "Dawn Knitting Worsted" was used for the original model.

MATERIALS: Knitting Worsted—or—Orlon yarn of Knitting Worsted weight. Main Color (MC)—12 (14-16-18-18) ozs; 1 oz each of colors A and B.
Knitting Needles: 1 pr each of No. 5 and No. 7 or size required to knit to gauge. 1 set of No. 5 dp needles.

GAUGE—The Most Important Word in Knitting
6 sts = 1"; 6 rows = 1".
Detailed drawings of how to make all of the basic stitches and all abbreviations used in these directions appear in the "How-To Section"—pages 169-210.

TEST PIECE: With No. 7 needles, cast on 19 sts. Work in pat for 18 rows. Piece should measure 3 × 3 inches. If too small, try larger-size needles; if too large, try smaller-size needles until correct gauge is obtained. While knitting, measure your work frequently to be sure you are maintaining the gauge.

MEASUREMENTS: Chest—26 (28-30-32-34)"; across back and front at underarms—13 (14-15-16-17)"; sleeve width at upperarm—10 (11-11½-12-13½)".

Ribbing—Row 1: P 1, * k 1, p 1; repeat from * across. **Row 2**: K 1, * p 1, k 1; repeat from * across. Repeat these 2 rows for ribbing.

PATTERN STITCH—Uneven multiple of stitches.
Row 1—right side: P 1, * k into back loop of next st, p 1; repeat from * across. **Row 2**: K 1, * p 1, k into the back loop of next st;
(Continued on p. 34)

repeat from * across. Repeat these 2 rows for pat. Always k into the back loop of each k st as it faces you.

BACK: With No. 5 needles and MC, cast on 79 (85-91-97-105) sts. Work in ribbing for 10 (10-12-12-12) rows. Attach A, k 1 row then work 3 rows of ribbing. Break off A. With MC, k 1 row then work 3 rows of ribbing. Attach B, k 1 row then work 3 rows of ribbing. Break off B. With MC, k 1 row then work 1 row of ribbing. Change to No. 7 needles. Work even in pat until piece measures 9 (10-11-12-12)" or desired length to underarms. End with row 2 of pat. Mark each end of last row.
Raglan Armholes—Row 1: P 1, p 3 tog, p 1, work pat across to last 3 sts, p 3. **Row 2:** K 1, k 3 tog, k 1, work pat to last 3 sts, k 3. **Rows 3 through 6:** Repeat rows 1 and 2 twice. **Row 7:** P 3, work in pat to last 3 sts, p 3. **Row 8:** K 3, work in pat to last 3 sts, k 3. Repeat these 8 rows until 23 (25-27-29-29) sts remain. Slip sts to a holder.

FRONT: Work same as back to underarms. Mark each end of last row and center st.
Raglan Armhole and Neck Shaping—Row 1: P 1, p 3 tog, p 1, work to center st. Slip center st to a safety pin, slip remaining 39 (42-45-48-52) sts to a holder for right front. Turn, work to arm edge, ending k 3. At neck edge dec 1 st every other row 9 (10-11-12-12) times and at arm edge work raglan decs same as right arm edge of back until 2 sts remain. K 2 tog. Leave center st on pin. Attach yarn, work across to last 3 sts, k 3. **Next Row:** K 1, k 3 tog, work to neck edge. Complete to correspond to left front, reversing all shaping.

SLEEVES: With No. 5 needles and MC, cast on 47 (53-55-59-65) sts. Work cuff same as lower edge of back. Change to No. 7 needles. Working new sts in pat, inc 1 st each side every 8th row 7 (6-7-7-8) times—61 (65-69-73-81) sts. Work even until sleeve measures 11½ (12-13½-14½-15½)" or desired length to underarms. Mark each end of last row.
Shaping: Work raglan shaping same as back until 5 sts remain. Slip sts to a holder.

FINISHING: Steam-press pieces lightly. Sew sleeves to front and back from marked rows to neck. Seam underarms and sleeves.

Neckband: With right side to you, using No. 5 dp needles and MC, pick up and k 5 sts across left sleeve; 20 (22-24-26-28) sts along side of neck; k center st; pick up 20 (22-24-26-28) sts along right neck edge; 5 sts along sleeve and 23 (25-27-29-29) sts across back of neck—74 (80-86-92-96) sts. Divide sts evenly on 3 needles. Attach A. Decreasing 1 st each side of center st every other rnd (always k center st), k 1 rnd A then rib 2 rnds. Repeat last 3 rnds with MC and B. Bind off loosely in ribbing.

Girl's Dress

shown on page 37
Sizes 4, 6, 8, 10

Directions are for size 4. Changes for sizes 6, 8, and 10 are in parentheses.
COLUMBIA-MINERVA "Velveen" was used for the original model.

MATERIALS: 3 Ply Fingering Yarn—11 (12-14-16) ozs. 5 small buttons.
Knitting Needles: 1 pr of No. 3 or size required to knit to gauge. Steel crochet hook No. 4.

GAUGE—The Most Important Word in Knitting
8 sts = 1"; 12 rows = 1".
Detailed drawings of how to make all of the basic stitches and all abbreviations used in these directions appear in the "How-To Section"—pages 169-210.
(Continued on p. 36)

TEST PIECE: Cast on 24 sts. Work in stockinette st (k 1 row, p 1 row) for 36 rows. Piece should measure 3 × 3 inches. If too small, try larger-size needles; if too large, try smaller-size needles until correct gauge is obtained. While knitting, measure your work frequently to be sure you are maintaining the gauge.

MEASUREMENTS: Chest—24 (26-28-30)"; across back and front at underarms—12 (13-14-15)"; sleeve width at upperarm—9 (9½-10-10¾)"; underarm seam—4½ (5-5½-6½)"; skirt length—11¾ (14-16¼-19½)".

PATTERN STITCH:—Multiple of 8 sts plus 1.
Row 1—wrong side: Knit. **Row 2:** K 3, * yo, sl 1, k 2 tog, psso, yo, k 5; repeat from *, ending last repeat k 3. **Row 3:** Purl. **Row 4:** K 2 tog, k 1, * yo, k 3, yo, k 1, sl 1, k 2 tog, psso, k 1; repeat from *, ending last repeat yo, k 3, yo, k 1, k 2 tog. **Row 5:** Purl. **Row 6:** K 2 tog, * yo, k 5, yo, sl 1, k 2 tog, psso; repeat from *, ending last repeat yo, k 5, yo, k 2 tog. **Row 7:** Purl. **Row 8:** K 2, * yo, k 1, sl 1, k 2 tog, psso, k 1, yo, k 3; repeat from *, ending last repeat yo, k 1, sl 1, k 2 tog, psso, k 1, yo, k 2. **Row 9:** Purl. **Row 10:** Repeat row 2. **Row 11:** Knit.

(Continued on p. 38)

Girl's Dress instructions are on page 35.

SKIRT

Skirt is planned for 11¾ (14-16¼-19½)" length. Make any adjustment in length before working lace panel.

BACK: Cast on 249 (265-281-289) sts. Work in stockinette st (k 1 row, p 1 row) for 11 rows. K next row on wrong side, working into back loop of sts for hemline. Continue until piece measures 3 (3½-4-5)" above hemline. End with a k row. Work rows 1 through 10 of lace pattern. **Row 11:** Knit, inc or dec to 250 (260-280-290) sts. K 1 row, p 1 row. **Dec Row:** K 11 (12-13-13) sts, * k 2 tog, k 23 (24-26-27) sts; repeat from *, ending k 2 tog, k 12 (12-13-14) sts—10 sts dec across row. Work even for ¾ (1-1-1)". **2nd Dec Row:** K 11 (12-13-13), * k 2 tog, k 22 (23-25-26); repeat from *, ending k 2 tog, k 11 (11-12-13). Work even for ¾ (1-1-1)". **3rd Dec Row:** K 10 (11-12-12), * k 2 tog, k 21 (22-24-25); repeat from *, ending k 2 tog, k 11 (11-12-13). Continue to dec 10 sts in this manner, having 1 st less between decs each dec row every ¾ (1-1-1)" 7 (1-4-10) times more; every ½ (¾-¾-1)" 1 (8-6-1) times—140 (140-150-150) sts. Work even until skirt measures 11¾ (14-16¼-19½)" or desired length. **Size 4 only**—k 2 tog 3 times; **Sizes 6-8-10**—k (5-1-7); **All sizes**— * k 2 tog, k 1; repeat from * across, ending last repeat k 2 (4-2-6). Bind off.

FRONT: Work same as back.

BLOUSE

BACK: Cast on 87 (93-101-107) sts. Work in stockinette st, inc 1 st each side every 10 (8-12-12) rows 5 (6-5-6) times—97 (105-111-119) sts. Work even until piece measures 4½ (5-5½-6½)" or desired length to underarms.

Armholes: Bind off 6 (6-8-8) sts at beg of next 2 rows. Dec 1 st each side every other row 2 (2-3-3) times—81 (89-89-97) sts. Work even for 2 rows, ending with a k row. Work rows 1 through 10 of pat. **Row 11:** Knit, inc or dec to 81 (85-93-97) sts.

Back Opening: K 40 (42-46-48), slip these sts to a holder; bind off next st, complete row. Work even on sts of one side until armhole measures 4¾ (5-5½-6)".
Shoulder: From arm edge bind off 7 (7-8-8) sts 3 times; 6 (7-7-8) sts once. Bind off remaining 13 (14-15-16) sts for back of neck. Attach yarn at center back and work other side to correspond.

FRONT: Work same as back, omitting back opening, until armholes measure 1½ (1½-1½-1¾)" less than back.
Neck and Shoulder: Work 30 (31-34-35) sts, slip these sts to a holder; bind off next 21 (23-25-27) sts, complete row. Working on sts of one side, dec 1 st at neck edge every other row 3 times. Work even until armhole measures same as back. From arm edge bind off 7 (7-8-8) sts 3 times; 6 (7-7-8) sts once. Attach yarn at opposite neck edge and work other side to correspond.

SLEEVES: Cast on 72 (76-80-86) sts. Work in stockinette st for 11 rows. K next row on wrong side, working into back loop of each st. Continue until sleeve measures 2 (2½-2½-3)" or desired length.
Shaping: Bind off 6 (6-8-8) sts at beg of next 2 rows. Dec 1 st each side every other row until 38 (38-30-24) sts remain. Bind off 2 sts at beg of next 10 (10-6-4) rows. Bind off remaining sts.

COLLAR—Make 2: Loosely cast on 70 (70-74-74) sts. Work in stockinette st for 1¼ (1¼-1½-1½)". **Dec Row:** K 7 (4-3-5), * k 2 tog, k 3 (4-4-5); repeat from *, ending last repeat k 6 (4-3-4). Work even for 5 rows. Dec as before, having 1 st less between decs. Work even until collar measures 2 (2-2½-2½)". Bind off.

FINISHING: Steam-press pieces lightly. Sew underarm, shoulder, sleeve, and skirt seams. Sew in sleeves. Sew bound-off edges of collar to neck edge meeting at center front. Hem sleeves and lower edge of skirt. Work 3 rows sc around waist edge of skirt. Work 2 rows sc around back opening, making 5 buttonloops along right edge. Work 2 rows sc around outer edges of collar. Sew skirt to blouse, easing in any fullness. Work a casing on wrong side at waist for elastic. Sew on buttons.

Slipon with Collar-Hood

shown on page 41
Sizes 4-6, 8-10, 12-14

Directions are for size 4-6. Changes for sizes 8-10 and 12-14 are in parentheses.
FLEISHER'S "Superior Knitted Worsted" was used for the original model.

MATERIALS: Knitting Worsted: 12 (16-16) ozs.
Knitting Needles: 1 pr each of No. 6 and No. 10 or size required to knit to gauge.

GAUGE—The Most Important Word in Knitting
6 sts = 2"; 18 rows = 2"
Detailed drawings of how to make all of the basic stitches and all abbreviations used in these directions appear in the "How-To Section"—pages 169-210.

TEST PIECE: With No. 10 needles, cast on 13 sts. Work even in pat for 18 rows. Piece should measure 4 × 2 inches. If too small, try larger-size needles; if too large, try smaller-size needles until correct gauge is obtained. While knitting, measure your work frequently to be sure you are maintaining the gauge.

MEASUREMENTS: At chest—28 (32-36)"; across back and front at underarms—14 (16-18)"; sleeve width at upperarm—11½ (13-14)".

RIBBING—Row 1—wrong side: K 1, * p 1, k 1; repeat from * across. **Row 2**: P 1, * k 1, p 1; repeat from * across. Repeat these 2 rows for all ribbing.

PATTERN STITCH—Multiple of 2 sts plus 1.
Row 1—right side: P 1, * k next st inserting needle into st in row below and knitting through both loops, p 1; repeat from * across. **Row 2**: K 1, p 1, * k next st, inserting needle in st in row below, p 1; repeat from * across, ending, k last st. Repeat these 2 rows for pat.

BACK: With No. 6 needles, cast on 43 (49-55) sts. Work in ribbing for 2½ (3-3)", ending with row 1. Mark first row of pat for right side of work. Change to No. 10 needles. Work even in pat until

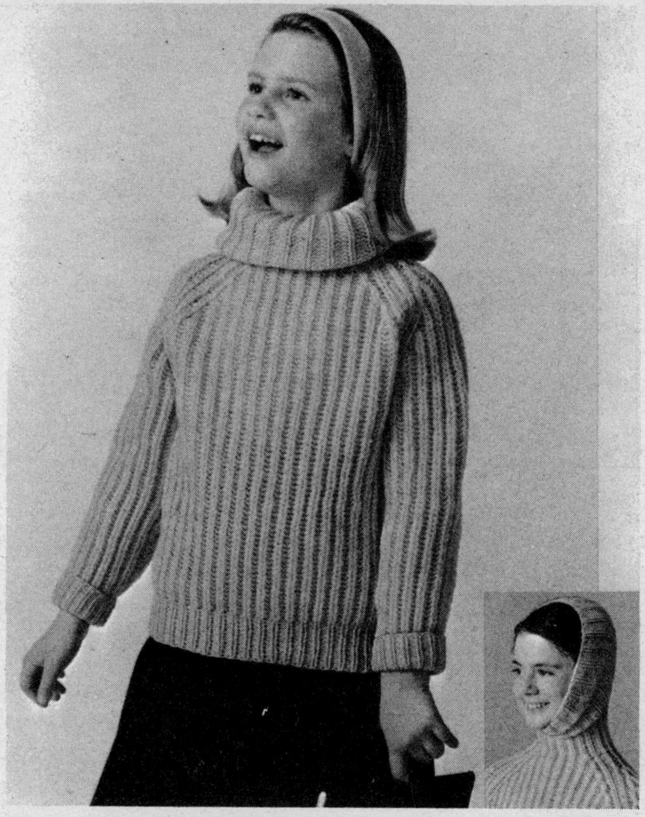

Slipon with Collar-Hood instructions are on page 40.

piece measures 8 (10-11)" or desired length to underarms. End with pat row 2 on wrong side. Mark each end of last row for underarms.

Raglan Shaping—First Dec Row: P 1, k into st in row below, p 1; sl next st as if to k, k 1, psso; work pat to last 5 sts, k 2 tog, p 1, k next st in row below, p 1—41 (47-53) sts. **2nd Dec Row:**
(Continued on p. 42)

K 1, p 1, k next st in row below, p 2 tog; work to last 5 sts, p 2 tog inserting needle from left to right in back of sts, k next st in row below, p 1, k 1—39 (45-51) sts. Work rows 1 and 2 of pat 3 times (no decreases). Repeat last 8 rows 6 (7-8) times more—15 (17-19) sts. Work even for 2 rows, ending on wrong side.
Collar-Hood: With No. 6 needles, continue in pat for 14 rows for neck. Change to No. 10 needles and continue for 9½ (10-10½)". Bind off very loosely in pat.

FRONT: Work same as back to Collar-Hood, ending on wrong side. Break yarn. Slip sts to a holder.

RIGHT SLEEVE: With No. 6 needles, cast on 31 (31-35) sts. Work in ribbing for 2 (2½-2½)", ending with row 1. Change to No. 10 needles. Work even in pat for 3 (2-2½)". Keeping continuity of pat, inc 1 st each side on next row and repeat incs every 3 (2-2½)" 1 (3-3) times more—35 (39-43) sts. Work even until sleeve measures 9 (11-12)" above ribbing or desired length to underarm. Mark each end of last row.
Raglan Shaping: Work same as raglan shaping on back until first dec row of last set of decs has been completed—9 sts. **Last Dec Row:** Work 3 sts, p 3 tog, work to end—7 sts. **Next Row:** P 1, k into row below, p 1, k into row below knitting through all loops, p 1, k into row below, p 1. Work even for 7 rows, ending on wrong side. Break yarn, place sts on a holder.

LEFT SLEEVE: Work same as right sleeve, ending on wrong side. *Do not break yarn*—7 sts. With No. 6 needles, work 1 row more, ending on right side. Leave sts on needle and yarn attached.
Sew raglan edges of front to corresponding raglan edges of each sleeve.

COLLAR-HOOD: Slip sts of right sleeve and front to free No. 6 needle. With right side to you, using needle with sts of left sleeve and yarn attached, pick up 1 st in raglan seam, work pat across sts of front, pick up 1 st in raglan seam, work across sts of right sleeve —31 (33-35) sts. Work in pat on No. 6 needles for 13 rows. Change to No. 10 needles and continue until same number of rows as back collar-hood. Bind off loosely in pat.

FINISHING: Sew raglan edges of back to sleeves. Sew collar-hood seams neatly. Sew underarm and sleeve seams. Steam-press lightly.

Knitted Ascot

shown on this page

BEEHIVE Imported Scotch Fingering Yarn, Patonized, was used for the original model.

MATERIALS: 3 Ply Fingering Yarn—or—Nylon and Wool Fingering: 2 ozs.
Knitting Needles: 1 pr of No. 2.

GAUGE—The Most Important Word in Knitting
8 sts = 1".

Cast on 3 sts. **Row 1**: K 3. **Row 2**: K 1, inc 1 st in next st, k 1. **Row 3**: K 1, inc 1 st in next st, k to end of row. Repeat row 3, increasing 1 st in 2nd st **every** row until there are 34 sts on needle. Work even in garter st (k every row) for 3".

Divide Sts—Next Row: * K 1, slip next st to a holder at front of work; repeat from * across—17 sts on holder and 17 sts on needle.

Slit—Cable Pat: Work 17 sts on needle. **Row 1—right side**: P 2, * k 3, p 2; repeat from * across. **Row 2**: K 2, * p 3, k 2; repeat from * across. **Row 3**: P 2, * sl 1, k 2, psso the 2 k sts, p 2; repeat from * across. **Row 4**: K 2, * p 1, yo (wrap yarn completely around needle), p 1, k 2; repeat from * across. Repeat these 4 rows for 2". End with pat row 2. Break yarn and slip these sts to a holder. Slip 17 sts from holder to needle so that the wrong sides of cable pat on slits will face each other. Work cable pat same as first section, ending on same pat row.

Joining Row: Holding first section at back of work, * k 1 st from needle, k 1 st from holder; repeat from * across—34 sts. Continue in garter st for 12" Work another slit in same manner as first slit. Join slits and continue until 3" from joining. **Dec Row**: K 1, k 2 tog, k to end of row. Repeat dec row until 3 sts remain. Bind off. Draw one end of Ascot through slit as pictured.

Designs 1 through 4 are knit from ***Basic Pullover*** directions, following individual charts. Instructions are on page 46.

Design No. 5—***Embroidered Cardigan and Headband*** instructions are on page 51.

Basic Pullovers

shown on pages 44-45
Sizes 4, 6, 8, 10, 12

Directions are for size 4. Changes for sizes 6, 8, 10, and 12 are in parentheses.
COLUMBIA-MINERVA "Knitting Worsted" was used for the original models.

MATERIALS: Knitting Worsted—or—Nantuk Knitting Worsted. Amount of yarn required for each pullover is given under each chart on pages 47 and 48.
Knitting Needles: 1 pr each of No. 6 and No. 9 or size required to knit to gauge.

GAUGE—The Most Important Word in Knitting
9 sts = 2"; 6 rows = 1".

TEST PIECE: With No. 9 needles and MC, cast on 18 sts. Work in stockinette st (k 1 row, p 1 row) for 18 rows. Piece should measure 4 × 3 inches. If too small, try larger-size needles, if too large, try smaller-size needles until correct gauge is obtained. While knitting, measure your work frequently to be sure you are maintaining the gauge.

MEASUREMENTS: At chest—24 (26-28-30-32)"; across back and front at underarms—12 (13-14-15-16)"; sleeve width at upperarm —12½ (13-13½-14-14½)"; sleeve seam—11 (11½-12½-13½-15)".

RIBBING—Row 1: K 1, * p 1, k 1; repeat from * across. **Row 2:** P 1, * k 1, p 1; repeat from * across. Repeat these 2 rows for all ribbing.
Note: When working designs and changing colors, always bring the color to be used from under and around the color just dropped; this will twist yarns and avoid a hole in work. Carry unused color loosely on wrong side of work. Read charts from right to left on k rows and from left to right on p rows, working "repeats" across.

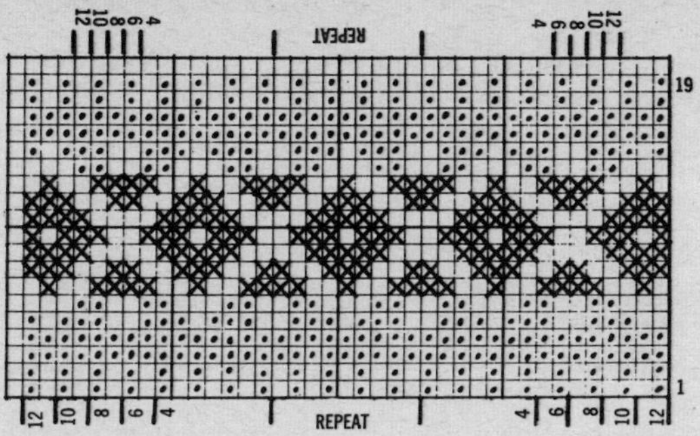

□ = A — 8 (10-12-12) ozs.; • = B — 2 (2-4-4) ozs.;
X = C — 2 (2-4-4) ozs.

DESIGN FOR PULLOVER No. 1: Start design 2 (4-6-8-10) rows above marked row at underarms. When design has been completed continue with A. Work neckband with C. **Sleeve Design:** Start design when 6 (6½-7-9-10)″ from picked up row or 5 (5-5-5½-5½)″ less than desired finished length of sleeves. **Cap:** Instructions are on page 50.

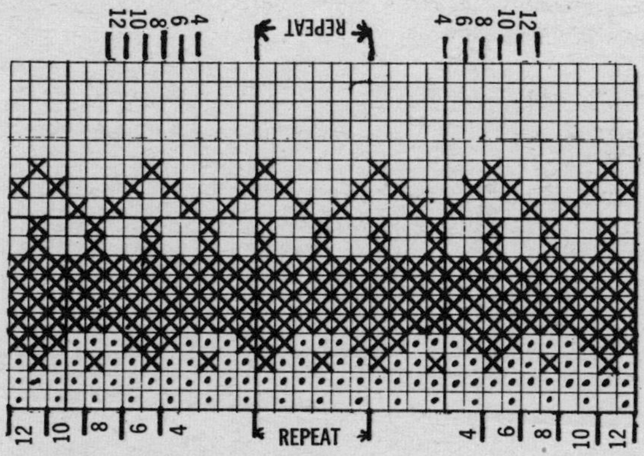

□ = Winter White (A) — 8 (10-12-12) ozs.;
• = Light Grey — 4 ozs.;
X = Blue, Moccasin, Gold — 4 ozs. of each color.

DESIGN FOR PULLOVER No. 2: Start design 2 rows above ribbing. Repeat rows 1 through 18, alternating the X sts of each stripe with a different color. If all X sts of each stripe are in same color, additional yarn of Color X is necessary, about 4 ozs. After last stripe worked just below shoulders, complete pullover with A. Pick up sleeves with A, p 1 row, k 1 row, p 1 row. Turn chart upside down and start chart at row 13. Work cuffs with A.

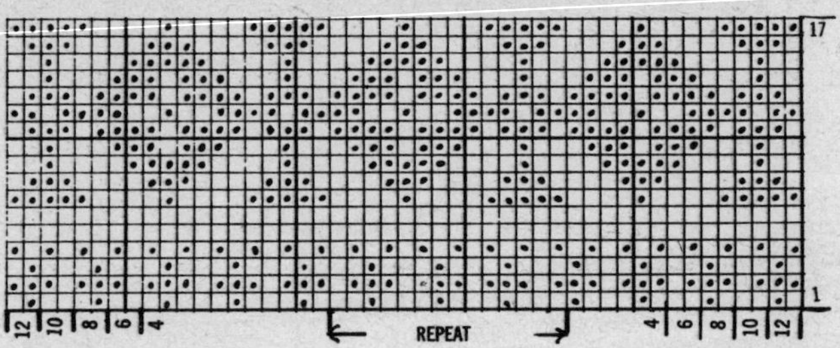

☐ = A — 8 (10-12-12) ozs.; • = B — 4 ozs.

DESIGN FOR PULLOVER No. 3: Start design 2 (2½-3-3½-4)" above marked row at underarms. Complete pullover with B.

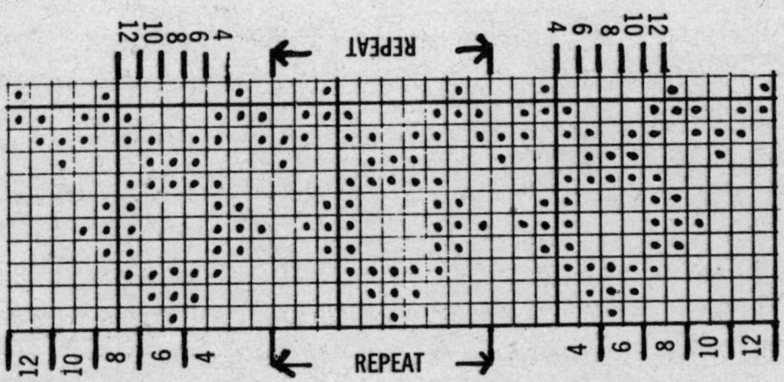

☐ = A — 8 (10-12-12) ozs.; • = B — 4 ozs.

DESIGN FOR PULLOVER No. 4: Start design 2½ (3-3½-4-4½)" above marked row for underarms. Complete pullover with B. **Sleeves:** Pick up sleeve sts with B, p 1 row, k 1 row, p 1 row. Turn chart upside down. Work rows 11 through 1 of chart and continue with A. Start decs after design has been completed. **Cap:** Instructions are on page 50.

PULLOVERS

FRONT: With No. 6 needles and A, cast on 55 (59-63-67-71) sts. Work in ribbing for 2 (2-2½-3-3)". On last row inc 4 sts evenly spaced—59 (63-67-71-75) sts. Change to No. 9 needles. Work in stockinette st (k 1 row, p 1 row) starting design for Pullover No. 2 as instructed. Work even until piece measures 9 (10-11½-11½-12)" or desired length to underarms. Mark each end of last row for underarms. Starting designs for Pullovers 2, 3 and 4 as instructed, continue until 5¼ (5¾-6¼-6¾-7)" above marked row.

Shoulders: Bind off 3 (4-5-6-7) sts at beg of next 2 rows; 5 sts at beg of next 4 rows—33 (35-37-39-41) sts.

NECKBANDS: Pullovers No. 1, 3, and 4 have a turned-under neckband. Pullover No. 2 has a double-ribbed neckband. Either neckband can be made.

Turned-Under Neckband: Change to No. 6 needles. P next row on right side for turning ridge and continue in stockinette st, inc 1 st each side every other row 4 times. Bind off.

Double-Ribbed Neckband: Change to No. 6 needles. Work in ribbing, dec 1 st each side every other row 4 times. Work even for 2 rows. Inc 1 st each side every other row 3 times. Bind off loosely in ribbing.

BACK: Work same as front. Seam shoulders and neckband edges.

SLEEVES: With right side to you using No. 9 needles and A (B for No. 4), pick up 57 (59-61-63-65) sts between marked rows of armhole. Work in stockinette st, dec 1 st each side every 6 (6-8-8-8) rows 7 times—43 (45-47-49-51) sts. Work even until sleeve measures 9 (9½-10½-11-12)" or 2 (2-2½-2½-3)" less than desired finished length. On last row dec 8 sts evenly spaced—35 (37-39-41-43) sts. Change to No. 6 needles. Work in ribbing for 2 (2-2½-2½-3)". Bind off loosely in ribbing.

FINISHING: Steam-press lightly. Sew underarm and sleeve seams. Turn neckband to wrong side and hem.

CAP No. 1

Sizes—Small, Medium, Large

With No. 6 needles and A, cast on 81 (91-99) sts. Work in ribbing for 3". Change to No. 9 needles. Work in stockinette st for 2 (4-4) rows, inc 2 (1-2) sts on first row—83 (92-101) sts. **Design**: Having 1 extra k st at each end of every row for seam st, work the 9 sts between the "repeat" of pat until chart has been completed. Break off B and C. With A, p 1 row. **Dec Row**: K 2, * k 2 tog, k 1; repeat from * across—58 (64-70) sts. P 1 row. **2nd Dec Row**: K 2 tog, p 2 tog across row. Change to No. 6 needles. K 1, p 1 in ribbing for 1 (1½-1¾)". Break yarn, draw end through sts, pull up tight and fasten securely. Sew back seam. Fold 1" of ribbing to wrong side and hem. Trim top of cap with a button.

CAP No. 4

Sizes—Small, Medium, Large

With No. 6 needles and B, cast on 81 (91-101) sts. Work in ribbing for 3". Inc 1 st at end of last row—82 (92-102) sts. Change to No. 9 needles. Work in stockinette st for 2 (4-4) rows. **Design**: Having 1 extra k st at each end of every row for seam st, work the 10 sts between the "repeat" of pat for sleeves until chart has been completed. Break off B. With A, continue in stockinette st until cap measures 6½ (7¼-8)" from beg. End with a p row, dec 1 st each side—80 (90-100) sts. **Dec Row**: * K 8, k 2 tog; repeat from * across. Work even for 3 rows. **2nd Dec Row**: * K 7, k 2 tog; repeat from * across. Work even for 3 rows. **3rd Dec Row**: * K 6, k 2 tog; repeat from * across. P 1 row. Repeat decs every k row, having 1 st less between decs each dec row twice more. End with a p row. Break yarn. Draw end through sts, pull up tight and fasten securely. Sew back seam, reversing one half of ribbing. Turn ribbing to right side forming a cuff.

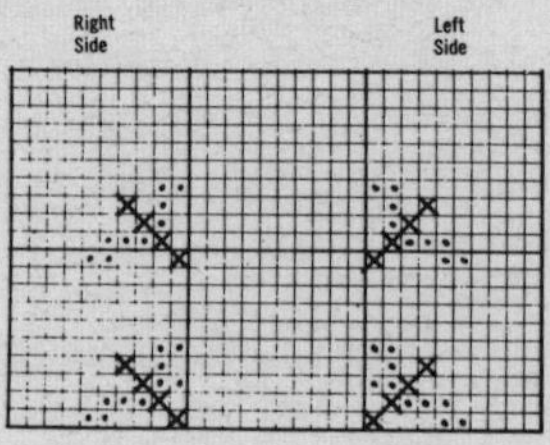

Embroidered Cardigan and Headband

shown as No. 5 on page 44
Sizes 4, 6, 8, 10, 12, 14

Directions are for size 4. Changes for sizes 6, 8, 10, 12, and 14 are in parentheses.
COLUMBIA-MINERVA Nantuk Knitting Worsted was used for the original model.

MATERIALS: Nantuk Knitting Worsted—or—Knitting Worsted: 10 (12-12-14-14-16-16) ozs. About ¼ oz of 2 colors for embroidery.

Knitting Needles: 1 pr each of No. 5 and No. 8 or size required to knit to gauge. Plastic crochet hook Size F.

GAUGE—The Most Important Word in Knitting
5 sts = 1″; 6 rows = 1″.
Detailed drawings of how to make all of the basic stitches and all abbreviations used in these directions appear in the "How-To Section"—pages 169-210.

TEST PIECE: With No. 8 needles, cast on 15 sts. Work in stockinette st (k 1 row, p 1 row) for 18 rows. Piece should measure 3 × 3 inches. If too small, try larger-size needles; if too large, try smaller-size needles until correct gauge is obtained. While knitting, measure your work frequently to be sure you are maintaining the gauge.

MEASUREMENTS: At Chest, buttoned—25 (27-29-31-33-35)″; across back at underarms—12 (13-14-15-16-17)″; across each front at underarms, border sts incl—7 (7½-8-8½-9-9½)″; sleeve width at upperarm—10½ (11-11½-12-12½-13)″.

TWISTED RIBBING—Row 1: K in back loop of first st, p 1, * k in back loop of next st, p 1; repeat from * across. Repeat this row for all ribbing.
(Continued on p. 52)

BACK: With No. 5 needles, cast on 60 (64-70-74-80-84) sts. Work in twisted ribbing for 2 (2-2½-2½-2½-3)". Change to No. 8 needles. Work in stockinette st (k 1 row, p 1 row) until piece measures 9 (10-11-11½-12-12)" or desired length to underarms.
Armholes: Bind off 3 (4-4-5-6-6) sts at beg of next 2 rows. Dec 1 st each side every other row 2 (2-3-3-4-4) times—50 (52-56-58-60-64) sts. Work even until armholes measure 5 (5-5½-6-6½-7)".
Shoulders: Bind off 4 (4-4-5-5-5) sts at beg of next 6 rows; 4 (5-6-4-5-6) sts at beg of next 2 rows. Bind off remaining 18 (18-20-20-20-22) sts for back of neck.

LEFT FRONT: With No. 5 needles, cast on 34 (36-40-42-46-48) sts. Work twisted ribbing same as back. Change to No. 8 needles. **Row 1**: K to last 7 sts, rib 7 for border sts (front edge). **Row 2**: Rib 7, p to end of row. Keeping 7 sts at front edge in twisted ribbing and remaining sts in stockinette st, work even until same length as back to underarm. End at side edge.
Armhole: Bind off 3 (4-4-5-6-6) sts at beg of next row. Dec 1 st at same edge every other row 2 (2-3-3-4-4) times—29 (30-33-34-36-38) sts. Work even until armhole measures 3½ (3½-4-4½-4¾-5)". End at front edge.
Neck and Shoulder: At neck edge bind off 9 sts once; 2 (2-3-3-3-4) sts once. Dec 1 st at same edge every other row 2 (2-3-3-4-4) times—16 (17-18-19-20-21) sts. When armhole measures same as back, from arm edge bind off 4 (4-4-5-5-5) sts 3 times; 4 (5-6-4-5-6) sts once.

Mark position of 8 buttons along border sts, having first marker in center of lower ribbing, 8th marker ¼" below neck, space 6 others evenly between.

RIGHT FRONT: Work to correspond to left front, reversing all shaping and making buttonholes opposite markers. **Buttonholes**: Starting at front edge, rib 3 sts, bind off next 2 sts, complete row. On next row cast on 2 sts over the bound-off sts.

SLEEVES: With No. 5 needles, cast on 34 (38-40-42-46-48) sts. Work in twisted ribbing for ½ (½-½-1-1-1)". Change to No. 8 needles. Work in stockinette st, inc 1 st each side every 6th row

9 times—52 (56-58-60-64-66) sts. Work even until sleeve measures 10 (10½-11-12-14-15)" or desired length.

Shaping: Bind off 3 (4-4-5-6-6) sts at beg of next 2 rows. Dec 1 st each side every other row until 30 sts remain. Bind off 2 sts at beg of next 6 rows. Bind off remaining sts.

FINISHING: Steam-press pieces lightly. Sew shoulder, underarm, and sleeve seams. Sew in sleeves.

COLLAR: With right side to you, using No. 6 needles and starting and ending in center of border sts, pick up 61 (63-65-67-69-71) sts all around neck edge. **Ribbing—Row 1**: Work twisted ribbing across, ending k in back loop of last st. **Row 2**: P 1, work twisted ribbing across. Repeat these 2 rows for 1". Change to No. 9 needles and continue until collar measures 2½ (2½-2½-3-3-3)". Bind off loosely in ribbing.

See chart on page 50.

EMBROIDERY: Following chart, embroider in cross sts, working over 1 k st, up each front about 1" from border sts. Work embroidery above ribbing on sleeves, spacing design evenly around.

HEADBAND

Sizes—Small, Medium, Large

With No. 8 needles, cast on 7 sts. Slip a marker each side of center st. Work in stockinette st, inc 1 st before first and after 2nd marker every k row until there are 43 (47-51) sts. Work even until piece measures 8½ (9½-10½)" or until band reaches from under chin to center top of head. Work second half to correspond, dec each side of center st to correspond to incs until 7 sts remain. Bind off. Gather sts along cast-on and bound-off edges. Fasten securely.

FINISHING: Steam-press lightly. With crochet hook, make 12" chain. Sl st in 2nd ch from hook, sl st in each st of ch; join to band at center of cast-on sts, continue in sc along edge of band to bound-off sts; make 2nd tie chain; continue in sc along opposite edge. Fasten off. Embroider sides of headband as pictured.

Four Piece Skating Set

shown on page 55
Sizes 4, 6, 8, 10, 12

Directions are for size 4. Changes for sizes 6, 8, 10, and 12 are in parentheses.
AMERICAN THREAD COMPANY "Dawn Knitting Worsted" was used for the original model.

MATERIALS: Knitting Worsted—or—Nylon and Wool of Knitting Worsted weight—16 (18-20-22-24) ozs. 2 ozs of Contrasting Color for trim. Zipper for back opening.

Knitting Needles: 1 circular needle No. 5; 1 pr each of No. 3 and No. 5 or size required to knit to gauge. Steel crochet hook No. 0.

GAUGE—The Most Important Word in Knitting
5½ sts = 1"; 8 rows or rnds = 1".
Detailed drawings of how to make all of the basic stitches and all abbreviations used in these directions appear in the "How-To Section"—pages 169-210.

TEST PIECE: With No. 5 needles, cast on 22 sts. Work in stockinette st (k 1 row, p 1 row) for 16 rows. Piece should measure 4 × 2 inches. If too small, try larger-size needles; if too large, try smaller-size needles until correct gauge is obtained. While knitting, measure your work frequently to be sure you are maintaining the gauge.

MEASUREMENTS: Chest—23 (25-27-29¼-31½)"; width of skirt at lower edge, approx.—66 (73-80-87-94)"; waist, approx.—18 (19¾-21½-23½-25)"; skirt length—8½ (9½-11-12½-14)"; sleeve width at upperarm—9 (9½-10-10½-11½)".

DRESS

SKIRT: Starting at lower edge with circular needle, cast on 360 (400-440-480-520) sts. Join, being careful not to twist sts. Mark beg of rnds. Work in rnds of stockinette st (k every rnd) for 3

(Continued on p. 56)

Four Piece Skating Set instructions are on page 54.

rnds. **First Dec Rnd**: * Slip a marker on needle, k 2 tog, k 16 (18-20-22-24) sts; repeat from * around—20 sts decreased. Slipping markers each rnd, dec 1 st after each marker every 6th rnd 5 (5-9-11-15) times more—240 (280-240-240-200) sts. Dec after each marker every 4th rnd 6 (8-5-5-2) times more—120 (120-140-140-160) sts.
Zipper Opening: At beg of next rnd, k 3, bind off next 2 sts for opening, k to bound-off sts—118 (118-138-138-158) sts. Turn. Work back and forth in stockinette st (p 1 row, k 1 row) for 3 rows. **Next Row—Sizes 4-8-12**: Dec 20 sts as before. **Sizes 6-10**: Dec 1 st after every other marker (10 sts dec)—98 (108-118-128-138) sts. Discard markers. Work even until skirt measures 8½ (9½-11-12½-14)" or desired length to waistline. End with a p row. Mark last row for waistline.

BODICE: K 23 (26-28-31-33) for left back, inc in next st, slip a marker on needle, inc in next st, k 48 (52-58-62-68) sts for front, inc in next st, slip a marker on needle, inc in next st, k 23 (26-28-31-33) for right back—4 sts inc. Inc 1 st each side of each marker every 4th row 6 (6-6-7-7) times more—126 (136-146-160-170) sts.
Sizes 6-8 only: Work even for 3 rows. On next row inc 1 st after first and before 2nd marker—126 (138-148-160-170) sts. Discard markers. Work even until piece measures 4½ (5-5½-6-6½)" above waistline or desired length to underarms. End with a p row.
Armholes: K 27 (30-33-36-38), bind off next 8 sts, k until there are 56 (62-66-72-78) sts on left-hand needle, bind off next 8 sts, complete row.
Right Back: With No. 5 straight needles, p first 27 (30-33-36-38) sts. Working on sts of one side, dec 1 st at arm edge every other row 2 (3-4-5-5) times—25 (27-29-31-33) sts. Work even until armhole measures 4½ (5-5½-6-6½)". End at arm edge.
Shoulder: From arm edge bind off 8 (8-9-9-10) sts once; 7 (8-8-9-9) sts once. Slip remaining 10 (11-12-13-14) sts to a holder for back of neck.
Front: With straight needles, work across 56 (62-66-72-78) sts of front. Dec 1 st each side every other row 2 (3-3-4-5) times—52 (56-60-64-68) sts. Work even until armholes measure 3 (3¼-3½-4-4½)".
Neck and Shoulder: Work first 21 (22-23-24-25) sts, turn. Working on one side, dec 1 st at neck edge *every* row 4 times; every other

row twice—15 (16-17-18-19) sts. Work even until armhole measures same as back. From arm edge bind off 8 (8-9-9-10) sts once; 7 (8-8-9-9) sts once. Slip center 10 (12-14-16-18) sts to a holder, attach yarn and work other side to correspond.
Left Back: Work to correspond to right back.

SLEEVES: With No. 5 straight needles, cast on 36 (36-38-38-40) sts. Work in stockinette st, inc 1 st each side every 8th row 7 (8-9-10-11) times—50 (52-56-58-62) sts. Work even until sleeve measures 10 (11½-13-14½-16)" or desired length.
Shaping: Bind off 4 sts at beg of next 2 rows. Dec 1 st each side every other row until 30 (30-28-28-26) sts remain; dec every row 8 times. Bind off remaining sts.

FINISHING: Steam-press pieces lightly. Sew shoulder and sleeve seams. Sew in sleeves. Press seams.
Neckband: With straight needles, k sts from left back holder; pick up 10 (11-12-13-14) sts along side of neck; k sts from front holder; pick up 10 (11-12-13-14) sts along other neck edge; k sts from right back holder—50 (56-62-68-74) sts. K 2, p 2 in ribbing for 1½". Bind off very loosely in ribbing. Fold neckband in half to wrong side and whip to inside neck edge. With Main Color, work 1 row sc around zipper opening. Sew in zipper.

BORDER: With Contrasting Color, sc around edge of skirt. Join with sl st in first sc. Do not turn. Working from left to right, sc in each sc around. Fasten off. Work border around edge of sleeves.

CAP

Sizes—Small, Medium, Large

With No. 5 needles, cast on 94 (98-102) sts. **Ribbing Row 1**: K 2, * p 2, k 2; repeat from * across. **Row 2—right side**: P 2, * k 2, p 2; repeat from * across. Repeat these 2 rows for 1½ (1½-1¾-1¾-2)". Work in stockinette st for 3 (3½-4-4½-5)". End with a k row. K next row on wrong side for folding ridge. Continue in stockinette st for 1½ (1½-2-2-2)". End with a p row.
Shaping: K 10 (8-10), * slip a marker on needle, k 2 tog, k 7 (8-8); repeat from * to last 12 (10-12) sts, slip a marker on needle, k 2 tog, k 10 (8-10)—9 sts dec. P next row slipping markers. **Row 3**: * K to marker, slip marker, k 2 tog; repeat from * ending k remain-
(Continued on p. 58)

ing sts. Repeat last 2 rows until 13 (17-12) sts remain. Break yarn. Draw end through sts, pull up tight and fasten securely. Sew back seam. Trim top of cap with big pompon. Fold ribbing in half to right side forming cuff if desired.

BRIEFS

Sizes 4, 6, 8, 10, 12

BACK: Starting at top with No. 3 needles, cast on 50 (54-58-62-66) sts. **Ribbing—Row 1**: K 2, * p 2, k 2; repeat from * across. **Row 2**: P 2, * k 2, p 2; repeat from * across. Repeat these 2 rows for 1¼ (1¼-1¼-1½-1½)". Change to No. 5 needles.

Short Row 1: K to last 3 sts, turn. **Row 2**: Sl 1, p to last 3 sts, turn. **Row 3**: Sl 1, k to last 6 sts, turn. **Row 4**: Sl 1, p to last 6 sts, turn. Continue to slip first st and to work 3 sts less at end of each row until there are 12 (12-15-15-18-18) unworked sts at each edge. **Next 2 rows**: Turn, sl 1, k to end of row. P across all sts. Work in stockinette st, inc 1 st each side every 6th row 6 (7-8-9-10) times—62 (68-74-80-86) sts. Work even until piece measures 8 (8½-9-9½-10)" at center. End with a p row.

Leg Opening and Crotch: Bind off 3 sts at beg of next 8 rows—38 (44-50-56-62) sts. **Row 1**: Bind off 3 sts, k until there are 14 (17-20-23-26) sts on right-hand needle, slip a marker in needle, p and k in next st, k 2, k and p in next st, slip a marker on needle, k to end of row. **Row 2**: Bind off 3 sts, p to first marker, slip marker, k 1, p to 1 st before next marker, k 1, slip marker, p to end of row. **Row 3**: Bind off 3 sts, k to first marker, slip marker, p and k in next st, k to 1 st before next marker, k and p in next st, slip marker, k to end of row. Repeat rows 2 and 3 until 22 (24-26-28-30) sts remain. End with a p row. There are 12 (14-16-18-20) sts between markers. Retaining markers, work even until piece measures 12 (12¾-13½-14¼-15)" from beg. Mark last row for start of front. Work even for 1". End with a p row.

Front Shaping: Inc in first st, k to marker, slip marker, p 1, k 2 tog, k to 3 sts before next marker, sl 1, k 1, psso, p 1, slip marker, k to last st, inc in last st. **Row 2**: Inc in first st, p to first marker, slip marker, k 1, p to st before next marker, k 1, slip marker, p to last st, inc in last st. Repeat these 2 rows until 2 sts remain between markers—32 (36-40-44-48) sts. Discard markers. Cast on 2 sts at beg of next 8 rows; 3 (4-5-6-7) sts at beg of next 2 rows—62 (68-74-80-86) sts. Work even for 1". Dec 1 st each side and repeat decs every 1" 5 (6-7-8-9) times more—50 (54-58-62-66) sts. End with a p row. Change to No. 3 needles. Work ribbing as back. Bind off loosely in ribbing.

LEG BANDS: With right side to you using No. 3 needles, pick up 74 (78-82-86-90) sts all along leg opening. Work in ribbing for 1½". Bind off loosely in ribbing.

FINISHING: Sew side seams. Fold all ribbing in half to wrong side, insert elastic and hem. Steam-press lightly.

(Continued on p. 60)

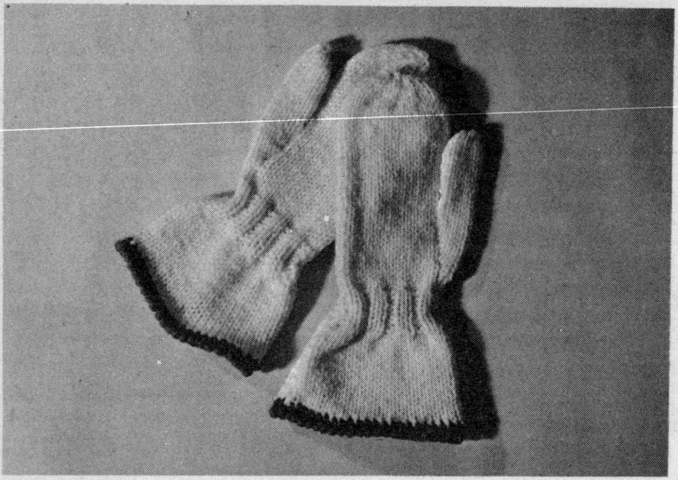

MITTENS

Sizes—Small, Medium, Large

LEFT MITTEN: With No. 5 needles, cast on 42 (46-50) sts. Work in stockinette st for 1½ (2-2½)". On last row dec 10 sts evenly spaced—32 (36-40) sts. Change to No. 3 needles. K 2, p 2 in ribbing for 1 (1-1½)". Change to No. 5 needles. Work 2 (4-6) rows stockinette st. End with a p row.

Thumb Gore and Thumb: K 14 (16-18), slip a marker on needle, p and k in next st, k and p in next st, slip another marker on needle, k 16 (18-20). **Row 2:** P to marker and slip, k 1, p to 1 st before next marker, k 1, slip marker, p to end of row. **Row 3:** K to marker and slip, p and k in next st, k to 1 st before next marker, k and p in next st, slip marker, k to end of row. Repeat rows 2 and 3 until there are 8 (10-12) sts between markers. Keeping the 2 p sts as established, work even until gore measures 1¾ (2-2¼)" from beg. End with a p row. **Next Row:** K 14 (16-18), k 8 (10-12) sts between markers, discard markers. Turn. Cast on 1 st, p 8 (10-12), cast on 1 st. Work even on 10 (12-14) sts of thumb, for 1¼ (1½-1¾)". K 2 tog across row; p 2 tog across next row. Break yarn, draw end through sts, pull up tight, sew thumb seam.

Hand: With k side to you, pick up 2 sts over thumb seam, k across 16 (18-20) sts of back of hand. P across 18 (20-22) sts and 14 (16-18) sts of palm—32 (36-40) sts. Work even until 2¼ (2½-3)" above picked-up sts. End with a p row.
Shaping: * K 2, k 2 tog; repeat from * across. **Row 2:** Purl. **Row 3:** * K 1, k 2 tog; repeat from * across. P 1 row. **Row 5:** K 2 tog across row. P 1 row. Break yarn, draw end through sts, pull up tight and fasten. Sew side seam.

RIGHT MITTEN: Work same as left mitten until 2 (4-6) rows above ribbing.
Thumb Gore and Thumb: K 16 (18-20), slip a marker on needle, p and k in next st, k and p in next st, slip another marker on needle, k 14 (16-18). **Row 2:** P to marker and slip, k 1, p to 1 st before next marker, k 1, slip marker, p to end of row. **Row 3:** K to marker and slip, p and k in next st, k to 1 st before next marker, k and p in next st, slip marker, k to end of row. Complete to correspond to left mitten.

FINISHING: With right side to you using CC, work 1 row sc around edge of mitten. Join with sl st in first sc. Do not turn. Working from left to right, sc in each sc around. Join and fasten off.

Argyle Slipon and Cardigan

shown on page 63
Sizes 4, 6, 8, 10, 12, 14

Directions are for size 4. Changes for sizes 6, 8, 10, 12, and 14 are in parentheses.
SPINNERIN "Nylaine Sport Yarn" was used for the original models.

MATERIALS: Orlon Sayelle of Sport Yarn weight: Main Color (MC)—6 (6-8-9-10-12) ozs; Colors A and B—2 (2-3-3-4-5-5) ozs of each color. 5 (6-6-7-7-7) buttons for cardigan.
Knitting Needles: 1 pr each of No. 4 and No. 6 or size required to knit to gauge.

(Continued on p. 62)

GAUGE—The Most Important Word in Knitting

6 sts = 1"; 8 rows = 1".

Detailed drawings of how to make all of the basic stitches and all abbreviations used in these directions appear in the "How-To Section"—pages 169-210.

TEST PIECE: With No. 6 needles, cast on 18 sts. Work in stockinette st (k 1 row, p 1 row) for 24 rows. Piece should measure 3 × 3 inches. If too small, try larger-size needles; if too large, try smaller-size needles until correct gauge is obtained. While knitting, measure your work frequently to be sure you are maintaining the gauge.

MEASUREMENTS: **Slipon**—Chest—24 (26-28-30-32-34)"; across back and front at underarms—12 (13-14-15-16-17)"; sleeve width at upperarm—9½ (10-10½-11¼-12-12½)". **Cardigan**: At chest, buttoned —25 (27-29-31-33-35)"; across back at underarms—12 (13-14-15-16-17)"; across each front at underarm, border sts incl—7 (7½-8-8½-9-9½)"; sleeve width—same as Slipon.

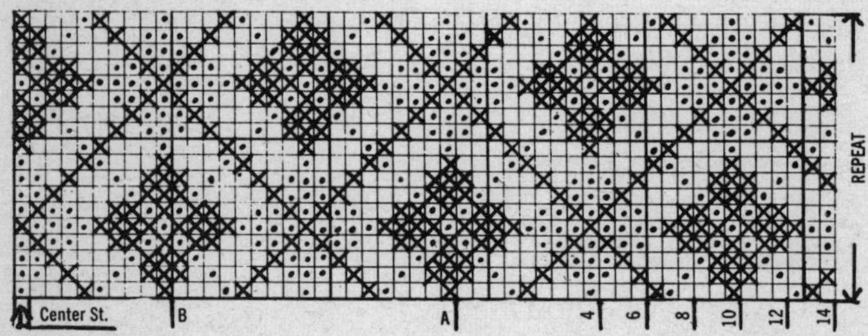

SLIPON: Reading chart from right to left on knit and purl rows, start at size indicated and work to B. Repeat between A and B across, ending as started.

CARDIGAN: Work back as Slipon.

Left Front: Start at size indicated and work to center st on knit rows. Work from center st to right on purl rows.

Right Front: Start at center st and work to right on knit rows. Work from size indicated to center st on purl rows.

(Continued on p. 64)

Argyle Slipon and Cardigan instructions are on page 61.

Note: When changing colors, always bring the color to be used from under and around the color just dropped; this twists yarns and avoids a hole in work.

SLIPON

BACK: With No. 4 needles and MC, cast on 72 (78-84-90-96-102) sts. K 1, p 1 in ribbing for 1½ (1½-2-2-2½-2½)". Inc 1 st at end of last row. Change to No. 6 needles. Work in stockinette st (k 1 row, p 1 row) following chart as instructed until piece measures 8½ (9-9½-10-11-12)" or desired length to underarms.

Armholes: Keeping pat sequence, bind off 6 sts at beg of next 2 rows. Dec 1 st each side every other row 4 (5-6-7-8-9) times—53 (57-61-65-69-73) sts. Work even until armholes measure 4¾ (5¼-5¾-6¼-6¾-7¼)".

Shoulders: Bind off 4 (5-6-5-6-7) sts at beg of next 2 rows; 5 (5-5-6-6-6) sts at beg of next 4 rows—25 (27-29-31-33-35) sts. Change to No. 4 needles. Break off A and B colors.

Neckband: With right side to you, k across all sts. **Ribbing—Row 1—wrong side**: K 1, * p 1, k 1; repeat from * across. **Row 2**: P 1, * k 1, p 1; repeat from * across. Repeat these 2 rows for 1". Bind off loosely in ribbing.

FRONT: Work same as back until armholes measure 2¼ (2¾-3-3¼-3¾-4¼)". End with a p row.

Neck and Shoulder: Work first 22 (23-24-25-26-27) sts. Turn. Working on sts of one side only, dec 1 st at neck edge **every** row 4 times; every other row 4 times—14 (15-16-17-18-19) sts. Work even until armhole measures same as back. End on same pat row. From arm edge bind off 4 (5-6-5-6-7) sts once; 5 (5-5-6-6-6) sts twice. Slip center 9 (11-13-15-17-19) sts to a holder, attach yarn and work other side to correspond.

SLEEVES: With No. 4 needles and MC, cast on 38 (40-42-44-46-48) sts. K 1, p 1 in ribbing for 2 (2-2-3-3-3)". Inc 4 sts evenly spaced on last row—42 (44-46-48-50-52) sts. Change to No. 6 needles. Work in stockinette st inc 1 st each side every ¾" 7 (8-9-10-11-12) times—56 (60-64-68-72-76) sts. Work even until sleeve measures 9 (10½-12-13½-15-16)" or desired length to underarm.

Shaping: Bind off 6 sts at beg of next 2 rows. Dec 1 st each side every other row until 28 sts remain. Bind off 2 sts at beg of next 4 rows. Bind off remaining sts.

NECKBAND: With right side to you, using No. 4 needles and MC, pick up 21 (21-22-22-23-23) sts along left neck edge; k 9 (11-13-15-17-19) sts from holder; pick up 21 (21-22-22-23-23) sts along right neck edge—51 (53-57-59-63-65) sts. Work ribbing as back neckband. Bind off loosely in ribbing.

FINISHING: Steam-press pieces lightly. Sew shoulder, underarm, and sleeve seams. Sew in sleeves.

CARDIGAN

BACK: Work same as for Slipon to neckband. Bind off 25 (27-29-31-33-35) sts for back of neck.

SLEEVES: Work same as for Slipon.

Note: Make front without buttonholes first—left front for girls; right front for boys. First buttonhole is made in center of waist ribbing, remaining buttonholes are worked later in front band. **Buttonholes**: Starting at either front edge, rib 2 sts, bind off next 2 sts, complete row. On next row cast on 2 sts over the bound-off sts. When spacing buttonholes on front band allow for last marker in center of 1" neckband.

LEFT FRONT: With No. 4 needles and MC, cast on 42 (46-48-52-54-58) sts. K 1, p 1 in ribbing for 1½ (1½-2-2-2½-2½)". On last row inc 2 (1-2-1-2-1) sts—44 (47-50-53-56-59) sts. Change to No. 6 needles. Work row 1 of chart as instructed to last 7 sts, slip these sts to a holder for front border. Continue following chart until same length as back to underarm, ending at side edge.
Armhole: Bind off 6 sts at beg of next row. Dec 1 st at same edge every other row 4 (5-6-7-8-9) times—27 (29-31-33-35-37) sts. Work even until armhole measures 2¼ (2¾-3-3¼-3¾-4¼)", ending at front edge.
Neck and Shoulder: Bind off 5 (6-7-8-9-10) sts at beg of next row. Dec 1 st at same edge *every* row 4 times; every other row 4 times —14 (15-16-17-18-19) sts. Work even until armhole measures same as back. End at arm edge on same pat row. From arm edge bind off 4 (5-6-5-6-7) sts once; 5 (5-5-6-6-6) sts twice.

(Continued on p. 66)

RIGHT FRONT: Work ribbing same as for left front, inc 2 (1-2-1-2-1) sts on last row, ending at front edge. Rib 7 border sts and slip them to a holder. Change to No. 6 needles, work row 1 of chart as instructed across remaining sts. Complete as left front, reversing all shaping.

BORDER STS—Work border without buttonholes first. **Left Front**: With right side to you, slip 7 sts to No. 4 needles. Work in ribbing until band reaches to neck edge when stretched slightly. Slip sts to a holder. **Right Front**: With wrong side to you, slip border sts to No. 4 needles. Work in ribbing to neck edge. **Buttonhole Border**: Work band the same, making 3 (4-4-5-5-5) buttonholes opposite markers. Sew bands to fronts.

FINISHING: Steam-press pieces lightly. Sew shoulder, underarm, and sleeve seams. Sew in sleeves.

NECKBAND: With right side to you, using No. 6 needles and MC, rib 7 border sts of right front; pick up 63 (69-71-77-81-85) sts all around neck edge to left front border sts, rib 7—77 (83-85-91-95-99) sts. Work in ribbing for 1", making last buttonhole when ribbing measures ½". Bind off loosely. Sew on buttons.

Mohair Eyelet Cardigan

shown on page 68
Sizes 4, 6, 8, 10, 12, 14

Directions are for size 4. Changes for sizes 6, 8, 10, 12, and 14 are in parentheses.
REYNOLDS "Mohair No. 1" was used for the original model. See chart on page 210 for comparable yarn.

MATERIALS: Mohair light weight—5 (6-8-8-9-10) ozs. 7 buttons. 1 (1-1¼-1½-1½-1½-1½) yds of ribbon for facing fronts.
Knitting Needles: 1 pr each of No. 5 and No. 8 or size required to knit to gauge.

GAUGE—The Most Important Word in Knitting
4½ sts = 1"; 11 rows = 2".
Detailed drawings of how to make all of the basic stitches and all abbreviations used in these directions appear in the "How-To Section"—pages 169-210.

TEST PIECE: With No. 8 needles, cast on 17 sts. Work in pat for 24 rows. Piece should measure 4 × 4 inches unstretched. If too small try larger-size needles; if too large, try smaller-size needles until correct gauge is obtained. While knitting, measure your work frequently to be sure you are maintaining the gauge.

MEASUREMENTS: Chest, buttoned—25 (27-29-31-33-35)"; across back at underarms—12½ (13-14-15-16-16¾)"; across each front at underarms—6 (6½-7-7½-8-8½)"; sleeve width at upperarms—9 (9½-10½-11½-12-12½)".

RIBBING—Row 1: K 1, * p 1, k 1; repeat from * across. **Row 2**: P 1, * k 1, p 1; repeat from * across. Repeat these 2 rows for ribbing.

PATTERN STITCH—Multiple of 6 sts plus 5.
Row 1—right side: P 5, * k 1, yo (wrap yarn completely around needle for this yo), p 5; repeat from * across. **Row 2**: K 5, * p 2, k 5; repeat from * across. There is 1 extra st in each pat. **Row 3**: P 5, * k 2, p 5; repeat from * across. **Rows 4 and 5**: Repeat rows 2 and 3. **Row 6**: K 5, * p 2 tog, k 5; repeat from * across. Pat is now restored to original number of sts. **Row 7**: P 2, * k 1, yo, p 5; repeat from * across, ending k 1, yo, p 2. **Row 8**: K 2, * p 2, k 5; repeat from * across, ending p 2, k 2. **Row 9**: P 2, * k 2, p 5; repeat from * across, ending k 2, p 2. **Rows 10 and 11**: Repeat rows 8 and 9. **Row 12**: K 2, * p 2 tog, k 5; repeat from * across, ending p 2 tog, k 2. Repeat these 12 rows for pat. Always count the 2 k sts on right side as 1 st. Accurate count of stitches can be made on rows 6 and 12. Work the 2 k sts on right side of pat as 1 st when binding off and decreasing.

Cardigan is worked in one piece to underarms.

BODY: With No. 5 needles, cast on 119 (125-137-143-155-161) sts. Work in ribbing for 1". **Buttonhole Row**: Rib 2 sts, work next 2 sts
(Continued on p. 70)

Mohair Eyelet Cardigan instructions are on page 66.

Crew Neck Pullover instructions are on page 71.

(Cardigan continued from p. 67)
tog, yo, complete row. On next row work the yo as a st. Continue in ribbing for 1", ending at buttonhole edge (right front). Remaining buttonholes will be the yo in the pat on each 7th row. Change to No. 8 needles. Work even in pat until piece measures 9 (9½-10-11-11-12)" or desired length to underarms. End with pat row 6 or 12. Tie a colored thread 31 (33-36-38-41-43) from each end of needle to indicate center of underarm.
Dividing Row: Starting at right front work row 1 or 7 to within 4 (4-5-5-6-6) sts of first marker (omit last yo if it falls within 6 sts of marker), slip these sts to a holder for right front—27 (29-31-33-35-37) sts not counting yo's; bind off next 8 (8-10-10-12-12) sts; work pat to within 4 (4-5-5-6-6) sts of next marker; slip remaining 35 (37-41-43-47-49) sts to a holder for underarm and left front.

BACK: Work row 2 or 8 of pat on 49 (51-55-57-61-63) sts. Keeping continuity of pat, dec 1 st each side every other row 15 (16-17-18-19-20) times—19 (19-21-21-23-23) sts. Bind off, working each k-2 as 1 st.

LEFT FRONT: Attach yarn at left underarm, bind off 8 (8-10-10-12-12) sts, complete row. Dec 1 st at arm edge every other row 9 (10-10-11-11-12) times. End at front edge.
Neck: From neck edge bind off 6 (7-7-8-8-9) sts once. Dec 1 st at neck and arm edge every other row 5 (5-6-6-7-7) times. Work 1 row, k last 2 sts tog.

RIGHT FRONT: Attach yarn at right underarm, work to front edge. Complete to correspond to left front, reversing all shaping.

SLEEVES: With No. 5 needles, cast on 23 (25-27-29-31-33) sts. Work in ribbing for 1 (1-1½-1½-2-2)". On last row inc 0 (4-2-6-4-8) sts evenly spaced. Change to No. 8 needles. Work in pat, inc 1 st each side every 1" 9 (7-9-7-9-7) times—41 (43-47-49-53-55) sts. Work even until sleeve measures 10½ (11-11½-12½-13½-14½)" or desired length.
Raglan Shaping: Bind off 4 (4-5-5-6-6) sts at beg of next 2 rows. Dec 1 st each side every other row until 3 sts remain, counting each k-2 as 1 st. Work 1 row. Bind off.

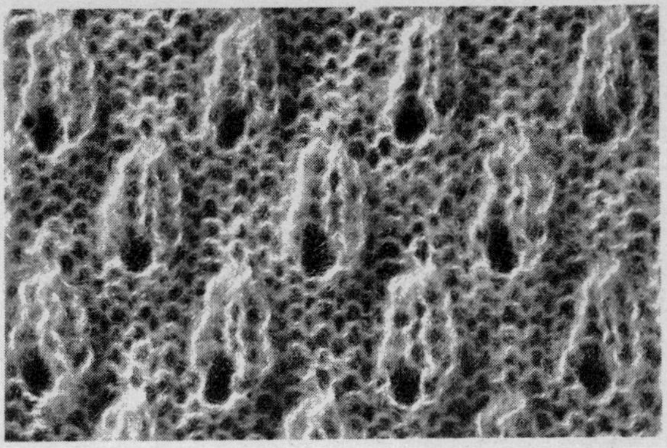

FINISHING: Steam-press pieces very lightly. Seam sleeves. Sew sleeves to fronts and back. Work 1 row sc along each front edge.

COLLAR: With wrong side to you, using No. 5 needles, pick up 63 (65-69-71-72-77) sts all around neck edge. Making another buttonhole on 3rd row, work in ribbing for 2½ (2½-2½-3-3-3)". Bind off loosely in ribbing. If desired, face fronts with 1" ribbon or nylon net. Clip under buttonholes and work tog with buttonhole st. Sew on buttons.

Crew Neck Pullover

shown on page 69
Sizes 4, 6, 8, 10, 12, 14

Directions are for size 4. Changes for sizes 6, 8, 10, 12, and 14 are in parentheses.
REYNOLDS "Versailles" was used for the original model.

MATERIALS: Sports Yarn—or—Sayelle Nantuk of Sports Yarn weight. Main color (MC)—8 (8-9-9-10-11) ozs; Color A—1 oz; Color B—2 (2-2-2-3-3) ozs.
Knitting Needles: 1 pr each of No. 5 and No. 8 or size required to knit to gauge.

(Continued on p. 72)

GAUGE—The Most Important Word in Knitting
4½ sts = 1"; 6 rows = 1".
Detailed drawing of how to make all of the basic sts and all abbreviations used in these directions appear in the "How-To Section"—pages 169-210.

TEST PIECE: With No. 8 needles and MC, cast on 18 sts. Work in pat for 24 rows. Piece should measure 4 × 4 inches. If too small, try larger-size needles; if too large, try smaller-size needles until correct gauge is obtained. While knitting, measure your work frequently to be sure you are maintaining the gauge.

MEASUREMENTS: Chest—25 (27-29-31-33-35)"; across back and front at underarms—12½ (13½-14½-16½-17½)"; sleeve width at uperarm—9½ (10-10½-11½-12½-13½)".

RIBBING—Row 1—right side: P 2, * k 2, p 2; repeat from * across. **Row 2:** K 2, * p 2, k 2; repeat from * across. Repeat these 2 rows for all ribbing.

PATTERN STITCH—Multiple of 4 sts plus 2.
Row 1—right side: P 2, * k 2, p 2; repeat from * across. **Row 2:** Purl. Repeat these 2 rows for pat.

BACK: With No. 5 needles and MC, cast on 54 (58-62-66-70-74) sts. Work in ribbing for 2 (2-2½-2½-2¾-2¾)". End with row 2. Change to No. 8 needles. Work in pat for 2". Inc 1 st each side every 1" 1 (1-2-2-2-2) times—56 (60-66-70-74-78) sts. Work even until piece measures 10 (10½-11-11½-12-12)" or 1" less than desired length to underarms. End with pat row 1. Change to Color A and continue in pat for 4 (4-4-6-6-6) rows.

Armholes: Change to Color B. Working 10 (10-12-12-14-14) rows of B, 4 (4-4-6-6-6) rows of A then completing back with MC, bind off 4 (4-5-5-6-6) sts at beg of next 2 rows. Dec 1 st each side every other row 2 (3-4-5-5-6) times—44 (46-48-50-52-54) sts. Work even until armholes measure 5 (5½-6-6½-7-7½)".

Shoulders and Facing: Bind off 5 (6-6-7-7-7) sts at beg of next 2 rows; 5 sts at beg of next 2 rows—24 (24-26-26-28-30) sts. Continuing in pat, inc 1 st each side **every** row 4 (6-6-8-8-8) times. Bind off loosely in pat.

FRONT: Work same as back.

SLEEVES: With No. 5 needles and MC, cast on 26 (30-30-34-34-38) sts. Work in ribbing for 2 (2-2-3-3-3)". End with row 2. Change to No. 8 needles. Work in pat for 1". Working new sts in pat, inc 1 st each side every ¾" 7 (7-9-9-11-11) times—40 (44-48-52-56-60) sts. Work even until sleeve measures 8 (8½-9½-10½-11½-13)" or 1" less than desired length to underarm, ending with pat row 1. Work 4 (4-4-6-6-6) rows A.

Shaping: Change to Color B. Working 10 (10-12-12-14-14) rows of B, 4 (4-4-6-6-6) rows A then completing sleeve with MC, bind off 3 (3-4-4-5-5) sts at beg of next 2 rows. Dec 1 st each side every other row until 22 (24-24-26-26-28) sts remain. Dec 1 st each side every row 4 (5-5-6-6-8) times. Bind off remaining sts.

FINISHING: Steam-press pieces lightly. Sew shoulder and facing seams. Sew underarm and sleeve seams. Sew in sleeves. Turn neck facing to wrong side and sew in place. Tack points of facings to shoulder seams.

Diagonal Striped Pullover

shown at left on page 75
Sizes 6, 8, 10, 12

Directions are for size 6. Changes for sizes 8, 10 and 12 are in parentheses.
COLUMBIA-MINERVA "Knitted Worsted" was used for the original model.

MATERIALS: Knitted Worsted—or—Nantuk Knitting Worsted: Main Color (A)—8 (8-10-12) ozs; Contrasting Color (B)—4 ozs for all sizes.
Knitting Needles: 1 pr each of No. 4, No. 9 and No. 10 or sizes required to knit to gauge.

GAUGE—The Most Important Word in Knitting
Pat St on No. 10 needles: 4 sts = 1"; 9 rows = 2".
Ribbing on No. 9 needles: 5 sts = 1"; 6 rows = 1".
Detailed drawings of how to make all of the basic stitches and all abbreviations used in these directions appear in the "How-To Section"—pages 169-210.

TEST PIECE: With No. 10 needles, cast on 16 sts. Work in stockinette st for 18 rows. Piece should measure 4 × 4 inches. Diagonal Stripe must be same gauge. With No. 9 needles cast on 14 sts. Work in rib pattern for 18 rows. Piece should measure 3 × 3 inches. If too small, try larger-size needles; if too large, try smaller-size needles until correct gauge is obtained. While knitting measure your work frequently to be sure you are maintaining the gauge.

(Continued on p. 76)

Diagonal Striped Pullover instructions are on page 74.
Triple-Cable Pullover instructions are on page 78.

(Pullover continued from p. 74)
MEASUREMENTS: Chest—26 (28-30-32)"; across back and front at underarms—13 (14-15-16)"; sleeve width at upperarm—10½ (11-12-13)".

RIBBING—Row 1—right side: K 2, * p 2, k 2; repeat from * across. **Row 2:** P 2, * k 2, p 2; repeat from * across. Repeat these 2 rows for all ribbing.

BACK: With No. 9 needles and A, cast on 50 (54-58-62) sts. Work in stockinette st (p 1 row, k 1 row) for 5 rows. P next row for turning ridge, inc 1 st each end of row—52 (56-60-64) sts. **Next Row:** With A, p 26 (28-30-32) sts, slip a marker on needle; p remaining 26 (28-30-32) sts. **Pat Row 1—right side:** K 1 B, * k 2 A, k 2 B; repeat from * across, slipping marker and ending k 2 A, k 1 B. **Row 2:** P 2 B, * p 2 A, p 2 B; repeat from * to within 2 sts of marker; p 4 A; ** p 2 B, p 2 A; repeat from ** across, ending p 2 B. **Row 3:** K 1 A, * k 2 B, k 2 A; repeat from * across, ending k 2 B, k 1 A. **Row 4:** P 2 A, * p 2 B, p 2 A; repeat from * to within 2 sts of marker; p 4 B; ** p 2 A, p 2 B; repeat from ** across, ending p 2 A. Repeat these 4 rows for stripe pat. Work even until 9½ (10½-11½-12½)" above turning ridge or desired length to underarms.
Armholes: Keeping continuity of pat, bind off 2 (2-3-3) sts at beg of next 2 rows. Dec 1 st each side every other row 3 (4-4-5) times —42 (44-46-48) sts. Work even until armhole measures 5½ (5¾-6-6½)" above bound-off sts.
Shoulders: Bind off 5 sts at beg of next 2 (4-4-2) rows; 4 (4-4-5) sts at beg of next 4 (2-2-4) rows. Bind off remaining 16 (16-18-18) sts for back of neck.

FRONT: Work same as back to underarms.
Armhole and Neck Shaping: Bind off 2 (2-3-3) sts at beg of next 2 rows. **Next Row:** Keeping continuity of pat, k 2 tog, work to within 2 sts of marker, k 2 tog; slip remaining 24 (26-27-29) sts to a holder. Working on sts of one side only, continue to dec 1 st at arm edge every other row 2 (3-3-4) times more and at neck edge dec 1 st every 4th row 7 (7-8-8) times more—13 (14-14-15) sts. Work even until armhole measures same as back.
Shoulder: From arm edge bind off 5 sts 1 (2-2-1) times; 4 (4-4-5) sts 2 (1-1-2) times more.

Attach yarn at center front on right side, k 2 tog, work to last 2 sts, k 2 tog. Complete to correspond to other side.

SLEEVES: With No. 4 needles and A, cast on 34 (34-38-38) sts. Work in ribbing for 2 (2-2½-2½)". Change to No. 9 needles. Keeping continuity of ribbing, inc 1 st each side every 6th row 9 (11-11-13) times—52 (56-60-64) sts. Work even until sleeve measures 12 (13-14-15½)" or desired length.
Shaping: Bind off 2 sts at beg of next 18 (20-22-24) rows. Bind off remaining sts.

NECKBAND: With No. 4 needles and A, cast on 8 sts. K 2, p 2 in ribbing until band when slightly stretched fits all around neck edge.

FINISHING: Steam-press pieces lightly. Sew shoulder, underarm and sleeve seams. Sew in sleeves. Pin center of neckband to center back of neck with ends at center front. Overlap ends forming a V and sew to neck edge.

BORDERED PULLOVER: *Continued from page 154.*

NECKBAND: With right side to you using No. 3 needles, pick up 26 (26-28-28-30-30) sts across back of neck; 6 sts across top of sleeve; 36 (40-40-42-44-48) sts along left neck edge; slip a marker on needle, k 2 sts from pin tog, slip a marker on needle; pick up 36 (40-40-42-48-48) sts along right neck edge and 6 sts across top of sleeve—111 (119-121-125-135-139) sts. Knit 1 row. K next row, dec 1 st each side of center st. Purl 1 row. Repeat last 2 rows once more. Work k 1, p 1 ribbing, always knitting the center st on right side and dec 1 st each side of center st every other row until there are 6 rows of ribbing. Bind off in ribbing, dec 2 sts as before. Sew right sleeve to back and neckband edges tog. Sew underarm and sleeve seams.

Triple-Cable Pullover

shown at right on page 75
Sizes 4-6, 8-10, 12-14

Directions are for size 4-6. Changes for sizes 8-10 and 12-14 are in parentheses.
COLUMBIA-MINERVA "Knitting Worsted" was used for the original model.

MATERIALS: Knitting Worsted—or—Nantuk Knitting Worsted: 12 (14-16) ozs.
Knitting Needles: 1 pr each of No. 5 and No. 9 or size required to knit to gauge. 1 set of No. 5 dp needles.

GAUGE—The Most Important Word in Knitting
11 sts = 2″; 6 rows = 1″.
Detailed drawings of how to make all of the basic stitches and all abbreviations used in these directions appear in the "How-To Section"—pages 169-210.

TEST PIECE: With No. 9 needles, cast on 18 sts. Work even in pat for 18 rows. Piece should measure 3⅓ × 3 inches. If too small, try larger-size needles; if too large, try smaller-size needles until correct gauge is obtained. While knitting, measure your work frequently to be sure you are maintaining the gauge.

MEASUREMENTS: Chest—27 (30-33)″; across back and front at underarms—13½ (15-16½)″; sleeve width at upperarm—10½ (12-13½)″.

PATTERN STITCH—Multiple of 8 sts plus 2.
Row 1—right side: P 2, * k 6, p 2; repeat from * across. **Row 2:** K 2, * p 6, k 2; repeat from * across. **Row 3:** As row 1. **Row 4:** K 2, * p 2, with yarn in front, slip next 2 sts as to p, p 2, k 2; repeat from * across. **Row 5:** P 2, * slip next 2 sts to dp needle and hold in back of work, k next st, k 2 sts from dp needle; slip next st to dp needle and hold in front of work, k next 2 sts, k st from dp needle,

p 2; repeat from * across. **Rows 6-9**: Repeat rows 4 and 5 twice. **Row 10**: K 2, * p 6, k 2; repeat from * across. **Rows 11-12**: Repeat rows 1 and 2. Repeat these 12 rows for pat.

BACK: With No. 5 needles, cast on 74 (82-90) sts. K 1, p 1 in ribbing for 1½ (2-3)". Change to No. 9 needles. Work even in pat until piece measures 10 (11-12)" or desired length to underarms.
Armholes: Keeping continuity of pat, bind off 5 sts at beg of next 2 rows. Dec 1 st each side every other row 3 times—58 (66-74) sts. Work even until armholes measure 5 (6-7)" above bound-off sts.
Shoulders: Bind off 8 (9-10) sts at beg of next 4 rows. Slip remaining 26 (30-34) sts to a holder for back of neck.

FRONT: Work same as b[illegible] until armholes measure 3½ (4½-5½)". End with a row on wron[illegible]e.
Neck and Shoulder Shaping: [illegible]rk across 18 (21-24) sts; slip next 22 (24-26) sts [illegible]older. Working on sts of one side, at neck edge dec 1 st every oth[illegible]ow 2 (3-4) times—16 (18-20) sts Work even until armhole measures same as back. From arm edge bind off 8 (9-10) sts twice.
Attach yarn at opposite neck edge and work other side to correspond.

SLEEVES: With No. 5 needles, cast on 34 (42-50) sts. K 1, p 1 in ribbing for 1½ (2½-3)". On last row inc 8 sts evenly spaced—42 (50-58) sts. Change to No. 9 needles. Work 12 rows of pat. Working new sts in pat as added, inc 1 st each side and repeat incs every 6th row 7 times more—58 (66-74) sts. Work even until sleeve measures 11½ (14-16)" or desired length.
Shaping: Bind off 5 sts at beg of next 2 rows. Dec 1 st each side every other row 9 (11-13) times. Bind off 3 sts at beg of next 4 rows. Bind off remaining 18 (22-26) sts.

FINISHING: Steam-press pieces lightly. Sew shoulder, underarm and sleeve seams. Sew in sleeves.
Neckband: With right side to you, using dp needles, pick up 66 (72-78) sts all around neck edge including sts on holders. Work around in k 1, p 1 ribbing for 3" or desired length. Bind off loosely in ribbing.

Cardigan and Slipon with Caps

shown on page 81
Sizes 4, 6, 8, 10, 12

Directions are for size 4. Changes for sizes 6, 8, 10, and 12 are in parentheses.
AMERICAN THREAD COMPANY "Dawn Knitting Worsted" was used for the original models.

MATERIALS: Knitting Worsted–Main Color (A)–10 (11-12-13-14) ozs; Contrasting Color (B)–5 (5-[illegible]6) ozs for Cardigan or Slipon and 1 Cap. 6 (6-6-7-7) but[illegible]for Cardigan.
Knitting Needles: 1 pr each of No. 7 and No. 10 or size required to knit to gauge.

GAUGE–The Most Important Word in Knitting
4 sts = 1"; 6 rows = 1".
Detailed drawings of how to make all of the basic stitches and all abbreviations used in these directions appear in the "How-To Section"–pages 169-210.

TEST PIECE: With No. 10 needles, cast on 13 sts. Work even in pat for 20 rows. Piece should measure 3 × 3¼ inches. If too small, try larger-size needles; if too large, try smaller-size needles until correct gauge is obtained. While knitting, measure your work frequently to be sure you are maintaining the gauge.

MEASUREMENTS: Cardigan–at chest buttoned–25 (27-29-31-33)"; across back at underarms–12 (13-14-15-16)"; across each front at underarms 7¼ (7¾-8¼-8¾-9¼)"; sleeve width at upperarm–10 (10-11-12-13)". **Slipon**–chest 24 (26-28-30-32)"; across back and front at underarms–12 (13-14-15-16)"; sleeve width–same as Cardigan.
Ribbing—Row 1: K 1, * p 1, k 1; repeat from * across. **Row 2:** P 1, * k 1, p 1; repeat from * across. Repeat these 2 rows for ribbing.
(Continued on p. 82)

Cardigan and Slipon with Caps instructions are on page 80.

PATTERN STITCH—Multiple of 2 sts plus 1.

Row 1—wrong side: With B, knit. **Row 2**: With B, k 1, * insert needle as to k into the loop of A st in front of and directly below next st, k this loop as a st, k next B st (1 st inc); repeat from * across ending k 1. Cut off B. **Row 3**: With A, p 1, * p 2 tog; repeat from * across, ending p 1. **Row 4**: K 1 A, * k 1 B, k 1 A; repeat from * across. **Rows 5 and 6**: With A, p 1 row, k 1 row. **Rows 7-8-9**: Repeat rows 1, 2, and 3. **Row 10**: K 1 B, * k 1 A, k 1 B; repeat from * across. Cut off B. **Row 11**: With A, p 1 row. **Row 12**: K 1 A, * k 1 B, k 1 A; repeat from * across. **Row 13**: With A, p 1 row. **Rows 14-15-16-17**: Repeat rows 10, 11, 12, and 13. **Rows 18 and 19**: Repeat rows 10 and 11. Do not cut B at end of row 18. **Row 20**: With A, k 1 row. Repeat these 20 rows for pat.

SLIPON

BACK: With No. 7 needles and A, cast on 49 (53-57-61-65) sts. Work in ribbing for 2 (2-2-2½-2½)". Change to No. 10 needles. Work even in pat until piece measures 9 (10-11-11½-12)" or desired length to underarms. Mark each end of last row. Continue in pat until 5½ (6-6¼-6¾-7¼)" above marker row.

Shoulders: Bind off 4 (4-4-5-5) sts at beg of next 4 rows; 4 (5-6-5-6) sts at beg of next 2 rows—25 (27-29-31-33) sts.

Neck Facing: Change to No. 7 needles and with A, p next row on right side for turning ridge. Continue in stockinette st (p 1 row, k 1 row) inc 1 st each side **every** row 7 times. Bind off loosely.

FRONT: Work same as back.

Sew shoulder seams and shaped edges of facing. Finish off all ends of yarn neatly on wrong side.

SLEEVES: With right side to you, using No. 10 needles and A, pick up 47 (49-53-57-61) sts along armhole edge between marked rows. **Row 1—wrong side**: With A, p 1 row. **Row 2**: Work same pat row as marked row at underarms and continue pat, matching body of slipon **below** marked row at underarms. Work even for 4 rows. Dec 1 st each side every 6th (6th-8th-8th-8th) rows 8 (7-7-6-8) times—31 (35-39-45-45) sts. Work even until sleeve measures 8½ (9½-10-11-13)" or 2 (2-2½-2½-2½)" less than desired length. Change to No. 7 needles and A. Work in ribbing for 2 (2-2½-2½-2½)". Bind off loosely in ribbing.

FINISHING: Sew underarm and sleeve seams, matching pats. Fold neck facing to wrong side and hem, catching ends of facing in shoulder seams.

CARDIGAN

BACK: Work same as back of Slipon to shoulders.
Shoulders: Bind off 4 (4-4-5-5) sts at beg of next 4 rows; 4 (5-6-5-6) sts at beg of next 4 rows. Bind off remaining 17 (17-17-21-21) sts for back of neck.
Note: Make front without buttonholes first—left front for girls; right front for boys. **Buttonholes:** Starting at either front edge, k 2, bind off next 2 sts, complete row. On next row cast on 2 sts over the bound-off sts.

LEFT FRONT: With No. 7 needles and A, cast on 29 (31-33-35-37) sts. **Row 1:** Work row 1 of ribbing across 23 (25-27-29-31) sts, k 6 (front border). **Row 2:** K 6, rib remaining sts. Repeat these 2 rows until ribbing measures same as back. End at front edge. Change to No. 10 needles. **Pat Row 1:** With A, k 6 border sts, attach B, k across. Always twist yarns when changing colors to avoid a hole in work. Keeping border sts in A, work remaining sts in pat until same length as back to underarm. Mark last row at arm edge and continue until 3 (3¼-3½-3¾-4)" above marked row. End at front edge.

(Continued on p. 84)

Neck and Shoulder: From neck edge bind off 6 (6-6-7-7) sts once; 2 sts twice; dec 1 st at same edge every other row 3 (3-3-4-4) times—16 (18-20-20-22) sts. Work even until armhole measures same as back. End on same pat row at side edge. From arm edge bind off 4 (4-4-5-5) sts twice; 4 (5-6-5-6) sts twice.

Mark position of 5 (5-5-6-6) buttons along border sts, having first marker in center of ribbing; space 4 (4-4-5-5) others evenly allowing for last button in neckband.

RIGHT FRONT: With No. 7 needles and A, cast on 29 (31-33-35-37) sts. **Ribbing—Row 1:** K 6 (front edge), rib across remaining sts. **Row 2:** Rib to last 6 sts, k 6. Keeping border sts as established complete ribbing, ending at side edge and making first buttonhole. Change to No. 10 needles. **Pat Row 1:** Attach B, k across to last 6 sts, attach a small ball of A, k 6. **Row 2:** K 6 A, pick up B, twist yarns, work row 2 of pat across. Complete to correspond to left front, reversing all shaping and making buttonholes opposite markers.

Sew shoulder seams. Finish off all ends neatly.

SLEEVES: Work same as sleeves of slipon.

FINISHING: Sew underarm and sleeve seams.

Neckband: With right side to you using No. 7 needles and A, pick up 65 (67-69-71-73) sts all around neck edge. Work in ribbing for ½". Make another buttonhole and continue for ½". Bind off loosely in ribbing. Steam-press lightly.

GIRL'S CAP

Sizes Small, Medium, Large

With No. 10 needles and A, cast on 72 (78-84) sts. K 1, p 1 in ribbing for 1¼". Work in stockinette st (k 1 row, p 1 row) for 6 (8-10) rows. **First Dec Row:** * K 10 (11-12) sts, k 2 tog; repeat from * across. P 1 row. **2nd Dec Row:** * K 9 (10-11), k 2 tog; repeat from * across. P 1 row. **3rd Dec Row:** * K 8 (9-10) sts, k 2 tog; repeat from * across. Continue in this manner, dec 6 sts every k row, having 1 st less between decs each dec row until 12 sts remain. K 2 tog across row—6 sts. Cut A and draw end through sts. Pull up tight, fasten securely and sew seam.

BORDER: With No. 10 needles and A, cast 71 (77-83) sts. K 2 rows. Work rows 7 through 14 of pat, then work rows 1, 2, and 3. Bind off with A. Sew short ends tog. Sew cast-on edges of border and cap tog matching seams at center back.
Pompon: Wind A and B together around a 5" cardboard about 25 times. Slip from cardboard, tie firmly in center. Clip loops and trim evenly. Sew to top of cap.

BOY'S CAP

Sizes: Small, Medium, Large

With No. 7 needles and A, cast on 71 (77-83) sts. Work in ribbing for 2". Change to No. 10 needles. Attach B, work in pat for 3¾ (4-4¾)". **Dec Rows**: Work dec rows same as girl's cap, having 1 st less in last repeat of each dec row (this will keep pat even—do not dec on rows 2 or 8 of pat) until 11 sts remain. **Last Row**: K 2 tog 5 times, k 1. Cut yarn and draw end through sts, pull up tight, fasten securely. Seam back. Turn up ribbing on right side.

Waffle Stitch Pullover for Him or Her

shown on page 87
Sizes 4, 6, 8, 10, 12, 14

Directions are for size 4. Changes for sizes 6, 8, 10, 12, and 14 are in parentheses.
BERNAT "Nylo Knitting Worsted" was used for the original model.

MATERIALS: Nylon and Wool of Knitting Worsted weight. Main Color (MC)—12 (12-14-14-16-16) ozs. Colors A and B—2 ozs of each color for all sizes.
Knitting Needles: 1 pr each of No. 8 and No. 10½ or size required to knit to gauge.
(Continued on p. 86)

GAUGE—The Most Important Word in Knitting
3 sts = 1"; 8 rows = 1".
Detailed drawings of how to make all of the basic stitches and all abbreviations used in these directions appear in the "How-To Section"—pages 169-210.

TEST PIECE: With No. 10½ needles and MC, cast on 10 sts. Work in pat for 16 rows. Piece should measure 3 × 2 inches. If too small, try larger-size needles; if too large, try smaller-size needles until correct gauge is obtained. While knitting, measure your work frequently to be sure you are maintaining the gauge.

MEASUREMENTS: At chest—25 (27-29-31-33-34)"; across back at underarms—12 (13-14-15-16-17)"; across front at underarms—13 (14-15-16-17-17)"; sleeve width at upperarm—9 (10-11-12-12½-14)".

PATTERN STITCH—Multiple of 2 sts.
Row 1: * K 1, k into st in row below; repeat from *, end k 2. **Row 2:** * K 1, p 1; repeat from * across. **Row 3:** K 2, * k into st in row below, k 1; repeat from * across. **Row 4:** * P 1, k 1; repeat from * across. Repeat these 4 rows for pat.

BACK: With No. 10½ needles and A, cast on 36 (38-42-46-48-52) sts. Work even in pat for 1¾". End with row 4 on wrong side. Attach B, work in pat for 2". End with row 4. Attach MC and continue in pat until piece measures 9 (10-11-11½-12-12)" or desired length to underarms.

(Continued on p. 88)

Waffle Stitch Pullover instructions are on page 85.

Raglan Armholes: Keeping continuity of pat, bind off 2 sts at beg of next 2 rows. Dec 1 st each side every 4th row 10 (11-12-13-14-15) times. Bind off remaining 12 (12-14-16-16-18) sts for back of neck.

FRONT: With No. 10½ needles and A, cast on 40 (42-46-48-50-52) sts. Work same as back to underarms.
Raglan Armholes and Neck Shaping: Bind off 2 sts at beg of next 2 rows. Dec 1 st each side every 4th row 7 (8-9-10-11-11) times. End with row 1 or 3—22 (22-24-24-24-[illegible]) sts. On next row slip center 6 (6-8-8-8-8) sts to a holder. Continuing decs at arm edge every 4th row 3 (3-3-3-3-4) times more, at neck edge bind off 2 sts once, dec 1 st every other row once. K last 2 sts tog. Attach yarn at opposite neck edge and work other side to correspond.

SLEEVES: With No. 8 needles and MC, cast on 24 (24-26-28-30-32) sts. K 1, p 1 in ribbing for 2 (2-2½-2½-3-3)". Change to No. 10½ needles. Attach A, work in pat for 1¾". With B, work in pat for 2". Continue with MC, inc 1 st each side every 1", 2 (3-4-4-4-5) times—28 (30-34-36-38-42) sts. Work even until sleeve measures 10 (10½-11½-12½-13-15)" or desired length.
Raglan Shaping: Bind off 2 sts at beg of next 2 rows. Dec 1 st each side every 4th row until 4 (4-6-6-6-8) sts remain. Bind off.

FINISHING: Steam-press pieces lightly. **Girl's Pullover:** Sew sleeves to front and back. Sew underarm and sleeve seams. Sew cast-on edge of collar to neck edge, centering at front. **Boy's Pullover:** Sew sleeves to front and one side of back. Work turtleneck collar then sew sleeve to back and collar edges tog. Sew underarm and sleeve seams.

GIRL'S COLLAR: With No. 8 needles and MC, cast on 77 (79-81-85-89-91) sts. **Row 1:** K 1, * p 1, k 1; repeat from * across. **Row 2:** P 1, * k 1, p 1; repeat from * across. Repeat these 2 rows for 4½ (5-5½-6-6-6)". Bind off in ribbing. Sew collar to neck edge.

BOY'S TURTLENECK: With right side to you, using No. 8 needles and MC, pick up 76 (78-80-84-88-90) sts all around neck edge. K 1, p 1 in ribbing for 4½ (5-5½-5½-6-6)". Bind off in ribbing.

Girl's Coat

shown on page 91
Sizes 6, 8, 10, 12

Directions are for size 6. Changes for sizes 8, 10, and 12 are in parentheses.
SPINNERIN "Orlon Sayelle" was used for the original model.

MATERIALS: Orlon Sayelle of Knitting Worsted weight—or—Knitting Worsted: 22 (25-28-31) ozs. 4 buttons. 1 yd of taffeta for facing.
Knitting Needles: 1 pr of No. 8 needles or size required to knit to gauge. Size F crochet hook.

GAUGE—The Most Important Word in Knitting
5½ sts = 1"; 7 rows = 1".
Detailed drawings of how to make all of the basic stitches and all abbreviations used in these directions appear in the "How-To Section"— pages 169-210.

TEST PIECE: Cast on 23 sts. Work in pat for 28 rows. Piece should measure 4 × 4 inches. If too small, try larger-size needles; if too large, try smaller-size needles until correct gauge is obtained. While knitting, measure your work frequently to be sure you are maintaining the gauge.

MEASUREMENTS: Chest at underarms (3" overlapped)—31 (33-35-37)"; lower edge (3" overlapped)—51 (53-55-57)"; sleeve width at upperarm—14 (15-16-17)"; length from underarm (1" hem incl)—17 (19-21-23)"; armhole—8 (8½-9-9½)"; sleeve length (1" hem incl)—13 (14½-16-17½)".

PATTERN STITCH—Double Moss St—uneven multiple of sts.
Row 1: K 1, * p 1, k 1; repeat from * across. **Row 2:** P 1, * k 1, p 1; repeat from * across. **Row 3:** P 1, * k 1, p 1; repeat from * across. **Row 4:** K 1, * p 1, k 1; repeat from * across. Repeat these 4 rows for pat.

(Continued on p. 90)

BACK: Cast on 143 (153-163-173) sts. Work in pat for 2". Keeping continuity of pat, dec 1 st each side of next row and repeat decs every 4th row 26 (28-30-32) times more—89 (95-101-107) sts. Work even until piece measures 17 (19-21-23)" or desired length to underarms, allowing 1" for hem.

Raglan Armholes: Bind off 5 sts at beg of next 2 rows. Dec 1 st each side every other row 28 (30-32-34) times. Bind off remaining 23 (25-27-29) sts for back of neck.

LEFT FRONT: Cast on 77 (83-89-95) sts. Work in pat for 2". End with row 2 or 4 at side edge. Dec 1 st at beg of next row and repeat dec at same edge every 4th row 26 (28-30-32) times more—50 (54-58-62) sts. Work even until same length as back to underarm. End at side edge.

Raglan Armhole and Neck Shaping: Bind off 5 sts at beg of next row. Dec 1 st at same edge every other row 21 (23-25-27) times—24 (26-28-30) sts. End at front edge. Bind off 9 (10-11-12) sts at beg of next row. Shape both edges at same time—at arm edge continue to dec 1 st every other row 3 times more and at neck edge bind off 6 (6-7-7) sts once; 5 (6-6-7) sts once. Fasten off remaining st. Mark position of 4 buttons 3½ (4-4½-5)" apart, having top marker about ¾" from neck edge.

RIGHT FRONT: Work to correspond to left front, having side edge at end of rows 1 and 3. Reverse all shaping and make buttonholes opposite markers. **Buttonholes:** Starting at front edge work 5 sts, bind off next 4 sts, complete row. On next row cast on 4 sts over the bound-off sts.

(Continued on p. 92)

Girl's Coat instructions are on page 89.

SLEEVES: Cast on 45 (47-49-51) sts. Work even in pat for 2". Keeping continuity of pat, inc 1 st each side and repeat incs every 4th row 15 (17-18-20) times—77 (83-87-93) sts. Work even until sleeve measures 13 (14½-16-17½)" or desired length allowing 1" for hem.

Raglan Shaping: Bind off 5 sts at beg of next 2 rows. Dec 1 st each side every other row 24 (26-28-30) times—19 (21-21-23) sts. **Left Sleeve**: Mark **end** of row 1 or 3 for front edge. Shape both edges at same time. At front edge bind off 4 sts 3 times; 2 (4-4-6) sts once continuing to dec 1 st at back edge of sleeve every other row 4 times more. Fasten off last st. **Right Sleeve**: Mark beg of row 1 or 3 for front edge. Complete as left sleeve reversing all shaping.

COLLAR: Cast on 25 (27-29-31) sts for back of neck. Work in pat, casting on 4 sts at beg of next 12 rows; 4 (5-6-7) sts at beg of next 2 rows—81 (85-89-93) sts. Inc 1 st each edge every 4th row 4 times—89 (93-97-101) sts. Work even until collar measures 4¾ (5-5¼-5½)" at center back. Bind off.

POCKETS—Make 2: Cast on 19 (21-23-25) sts. Work in pat, inc 1 st each side **every** row 3 times—25 (27-29-31) sts. Work even until piece measures 5½ (5¾-6-6¼)". Bind off in pat.

FINISHING: Steam-press pieces lightly. Sew back edges of sleeves to back of coat. Sew fronts to front edges of sleeves from underarms to bound-off sts at shaping. Sew underarm and sleeve seams. Turn a 1" hem at lower edge of coat, sleeves and top of pockets to wrong side and hem. With right side to you starting at lower right hem edge, work 1 row sc to neck edge, spacing sts to keep work flat, 3 sc in corner, continue around neck edge and down left front. Fasten off. Work 1 row sc around 3 edges of pockets and along narrow and bound-off edges of collar. Cut taffeta to fit pockets and collar. Turn in ¼" around lining and sew, leaving sc edge unlined. Cut 2 strips of taffeta about 3½" wide and 1" longer than coat from hemline to neck edge. Turn in ¼" and sew in place along fronts inside of sc rows. Cut buttonholes in facing under buttonholes on right front and overcast to buttonholes in coat. With center back of collar to center back of neck, starting and ending 1½" from front edges pin then sew collar in place. Sew on buttons. Steam-press seams and all edges again.

Mohair Raglan Pullover and Shell

shown at left on page 95
Sizes 4-6, 8-10, 12-14

Directions are for size 4-6. Changes for sizes 8-10 and 12-14 are in parentheses.

BEAR BRAND "Supra Mohair" and "Spice" were used for the original models. See chart on page 210 for comparable yarns.

MATERIALS: Mohair (50-gram ball)—7 (9-10) balls. Sports Yarn for Shell—4 (4-6) ozs.
Knitting Needles: 1 pr each of No. 6, No. 9, and No. 10 or sizes required to knit to gauge.

GAUGE—The Most Important Word in Knitting
On No. 10 needles—4 sts = 1"; 5 rows = 1".
On No. 9 needles—9 sts = 2"; 6 rows = 1".
Detailed drawings of how to make all of the basic stitches and all abbreviations used in these directions appear in the "How-To Section"—pages 169-210.

TEST PIECE: With No. 10 needles and Mohair, cast on 16 sts. Work in stockinette st (k 1 row, p 1 row) for 20 rows. Piece should measure 4 × 4 inches. With Knitting Worsted and No. 9 needles, cast on 18 sts. Work in stockinette st for 24 rows. Piece should measure 4 × 4 inches. If too small, try larger-size needles; if too large, try smaller-size needles until correct gauge is obtained. While knitting, measure your work frequently to be sure you are maintaining the gauge.

MEASUREMENTS: **Pullover**—Chest—26 (30-34)"; across back at underarms—12½ (14½-16½)"; across front at underarms—13½ (15½-17½)"; sleeve width at upperarm—10½ (12-13)". **Shell:** Chest—25 (29-33)".
Ribbing—Row 1—right side: P 1, * k 1, p 1; repeat from * across. **Row 2:** K 1, * p 1, k 1; repeat from * across. Repeat these 2 rows for ribbing.
(Continued on p. 94)

CABLE PATTERN—Multiple of 15 sts.
Row 1—right side: P 1, k 6, p 1, k 6, p 1. **Row 2:** K 1, p 6, k 1, p 6, k 1. **Rows 3 and 4:** Repeat rows 1 and 2. **Row 5:** P 1, slip next 3 sts to dp needle and hold in *back* of work, k next 3 sts, k 3 sts from dp needle; p 1; slip next 3 sts to dp needle and hold in *front* of work, k next 3 sts, k 3 sts from dp needle, p 1. **Row 6:** Repeat row 2. **Rows 7 and 8:** Repeat rows 1 and 2. Repeat these 8 rows for pat.

PULLOVER

BACK: With No. 6 needles and Mohair, cast on 49 (57-65) sts. Work in ribbing for 2 (2½-2½)". Inc 1 st each end of last row—51 (59-67) sts. Change to No. 10 needles. Work in stockinette st (k 1 row, p 1 row) until piece measures 8 (10-12)" or desired length to underarms. End with a p row.
Raglan Armholes: Bind off 1 (2-2) sts at beg of next 2 rows. Dec 1 st each side every other row 14 (16-18) times. Bind off remaining 21 (23-27) sts.

FRONT: With No. 6 needles, cast on 51 (59-65) sts. Work ribbing same as for back. On last row inc 4 sts evenly spaced—55 (63-69) sts. Change to No. 10 needles. **Pat Row 1:** K 20 (24-27) sts; work row 1 of cable pat across next 15 sts; k 20 (24-27) sts. **Row 2:** P 20 (24-27); work row 2 of cable pat across next 15 sts; p 20 (24-27) sts. Continue in this manner, working cable pat on center 15 sts until same length as back to underarms. End with a p row.
Raglan Armholes: Bind off 1 (2-2) sts at beg of next 2 rows. Dec 1 st each side every other row 3 (4-5) times—47 (51-55) sts. End with a k row.

(Continued on p. 96)

Mohair Raglan Pullover and Shell instructions are on page 93.
Mohair Cabled Cardigan instructions are on page 97.

Neck Shaping: On next row work 23 (25-27) sts, slip these sts to a holder; complete row on 24 (26-28) sts. Working on sts of left side of front and keeping continuity of cable pat on 8 sts at front edge, dec 1 st inside of border sts every 4th row 5 (6-7) times, continuing decs at raglan edge every other row until 8 border sts remain. Continue on border sts until band reaches to center back of neck. Bind off.

Right Front: Attach yarn at center front, inc 1 st, and complete to correspond to left front, reversing all shaping.

SLEEVES: With No. 6 needles, cast on 25 (29-31) sts. Work in ribbing for 2½ (3-3)". On last row inc 5 sts evenly spaced—30 (34-36) sts. Change to No. 10 needles. Work in stockinette st, inc 1 st each side every 1" 6 (7-8) times—42 (48-52) sts. Work even until sleeve measures 10 (12½-15)" or desired length.

Raglan Shaping: Work same as raglan armhole for back until 12 sts remain. Bind off.

FINISHING: Steam-press pieces lightly. Sew sleeves to front and back. Sew underarm and sleeve seams. Sew border ends tog, then sew border along top of sleeves and back of neck, adjusting to fit.

SHELL

BACK: With No. 6 needles and Knitting Worsted, cast on 57 (65-75) sts. Work in ribbing for 2 (2¼-2½)". Change to No. 9 needles. Work in stockinette st until 4 (6-7½)" above ribbing. End with a p row. **Border Sts—Row 1:** K 1, p 1 in ribbing across 10 (12-14) sts; k 37 (41-47) sts, p 1, k 1 to end of row. **Row 2:** P 1, k 1 in ribbing across 10 (12-14) sts; p 37 (41-47) sts, k 1, p 1 in ribbing to end of row. Repeat these 2 rows twice.

Armholes: Bind off 4 (6-8) sts at beg of next 2 rows—49 (53-59) sts. Keeping 6 sts each side in ribbing, work even until 5 (5½-6)" above armhole.

Shoulders and Neckband: Bind off 5 sts at beg of next 4 rows; 4 (5-7) sts at beg of next 2 rows. Change to No. 6 needles. Work in ribbing on 21 (23-25) sts for 1". Change to No. 9 needles and continue ribbing until neckband measures 3½ (4-4½)". Bind off loosely in ribbing.

FRONT: Work same as for back until armholes measure 4 (4½-5)".

Neck and Shoulder: Work 17 (18-20) sts; slip center 15 (17-19) sts to a holder. Working on sts of one side and keeping armhole edge even, at neck edge dec 1 st every other row 3 times—14 (15-17) sts. Work even until armhole measures same as back. From arm edge bind off 5 sts twice; 4 (5-7) sts once. Attach yarn at opposite neck edge and work other side to correspond.

Neckband: With right side to you, using No. 6 needles, pick up 12 sts along side of neck, k 15 (17-19) sts from holder; pick up 12 sts along right neck edge—39 (41-43) sts. Work ribbing same as for back neckband.

FINISHING: Steam-press pieces lightly. Do not press out ribbing. Sew underarm and shoulder seams. Sew neckband edges together, having seam underneath turnover collar. If desired work 1 row single crochet around armholes.

Mohair Cabled Cardigan

shown at right on page 95
Sizes 4-6, 8-10, 12-14

Directions are for size 4-6. Changes for sizes 8-10 and 12-14 are in parentheses.

BUCILLA "Mist-Aire" was used for the original model. See chart on page 210 for comparable yarns.

MATERIALS: Mohair (50-gram ball)—6 (7-8) balls: 6 (7-8) buttons.

Knitting Needles: 1 pr each of No. 5 and No. 8 or size required to knit to gauge.

GAUGE—The Most Important Word in Knitting
9 sts = 2"; 6 rows = 1".

Detailed drawing of how to make all of the basic stitches and all abbreviations used in these directions appear in the "How-To Section"—pages 169-210.

TEST PIECE: With No. 8 needles, cast on 18 sts. Work in stockinette st (k 1 row, p 1 row) for 18 rows. Piece should measure 4 × 3

(Continued on p. 98)

inches. If too small, try larger-size needles; if too large, try smaller-size needles until correct gauge is obtained. While knitting, measure your work frequently to be sure you are maintaining the gauge.

MEASUREMENTS: At chest, buttoned—28 (32-35)"; across back at underarms—14 (15½-17½)"; sleeve width at upperarm—11½ (13-15)".
Cardigan is worked from collar down.

COLLAR: With No. 8 needles, cast on 63 sts. **Ribbing—Row 1—wrong side**: K 1, * p 1, k 1; repeat from * across. **Row 2**: P 1, * k 1, p 1; repeat from * across. Repeat these 2 rows for 2½ (3-3)". End with row 1. **Next Row**: Continuing ribbing, work 15 sts for right front, slip a marker on needle; work 8 sts for sleeve, slip a marker on needle; work 18 sts for back, slip a marker on needle; work 8 sts for sleeve, slip a marker on needle; work 14 sts for left front. **Raglan Shaping—Row 1—right side**: Rib to within 1 st of marker, inc in next st as to k, slip marker, inc in next st as to k, * p 1, k 1 in ribbing to within 1 st of next marker, inc in next st as to k, slip marker, inc in next st as to k; repeat from * twice more, p 1, k 1 to end of row—71 sts. **Row 2**: * Rib to within 2 sts of marker, p 2, slip marker, p 1; repeat from * 3 times more, rib to end of row. **Row 3**: Rib across, inc 1 st each side of each marker—79 sts. **Row 4**: Work as row 2. Repeat rows 1 and 2 once more—87 sts. Carry markers and slip them every row.

Raglan Yoke—Row 7: Rib 6 for left front border sts, k 4, inc in each of next 2 sts, k 4, inc 1 st in each of next 2 sts, * k to within 1 st of next marker, inc in each of next 2 sts; repeat from * twice more, k 5, inc in next st, k 5, rib 6 for right front border sts, 98 sts. **Row 8:** Rib 6, p 12, k 1; p to last 19 sts, k 1, p 12, rib 6. **Row 9—Cable Row:** Rib 6, slip next 3 sts to dp needle and hold in *front* of work, k next 3 sts, k 3 sts from dp needle; slip next 3 sts to dp needle and hold in *back* of work, k next 3 sts, k 3 sts from dp needle (double cable made), p 1; inc in each of next 2 sts, * k to within 1 st of next marker, inc in next 2 sts; repeat from * twice, p 1, make double cable over next 12 sts, rib 6—106 sts. **Row 10:** As row 8. **Row 11:** Rib 6, k 12, p 1, k 1, inc in next 2 sts, * k to within 1 st of next marker, inc in next 2 sts; repeat from * twice, k 1, p 1, k 12, rib 6—114 sts. **Row 12:** As row 8. Keeping 19 sts at each edge in border sts and cable pat as established, continue to inc 1 st each side of each marker every other row twice more—130 sts. **Row 17—Buttonhole Row:** Rib 6, work double cable over next 12 sts, p 1; work across, inc 1 st each side of markers to last 19 sts, p 1, work double cable over next 12 sts, p 1, k 1, bind off next 2 sts, complete row. On next row cast on 2 sts over the bound-off sts—138 sts. Continue in this manner, inc 1 st each side of each marker every other row 11 (15-19) times more, taking care to cable every 8th row and repeating buttonholes every 15th and 16th rows. End at right front edge—226 (258-290) sts. Remove markers.

Dividing Row: Work 36 (40-44) sts, slip these sts to a holder for right front; work next 48 (56-64) sts and slip them to a holder for right sleeve; work 58 (66-74) sts, slip them to a holder for back; work next 48 (56-64) sts for sleeve; slip remaining 36 (40-44) sts to a holder for left front.

LEFT SLEEVE: Continuing in stockinette st, cast on 2 sts at beg of next 2 rows—52 (60-68) sts. Work even for 4 rows. Dec 1 st each side of next row and repeat decs every 4th row 1 (2-3) times; every 6th row 6 (7-8) times—36 (40-44) sts. Work even until sleeve measures 10 (11½-13½)" from underarm or 2 (2½-2½)" less than desired finished length. On last row dec 6 sts evenly spaced—30 (34-38) sts. K 1, p 1 in ribbing for 2 (2½-2½)". Bind off loosely in ribbing.

(Continued on p. 100)

RIGHT SLEEVE: Work to correspond to left sleeve. Seam sleeves.

BODY: Starting at underarm of left front, work to front edge. **Joining Row—right side:** Work 36 (40-44) sts of left front, pick up 4 sts over cast-on sts of sleeve; k 58 (66-74) sts of back; pick up 4 sts over cast-on sts of sleeve; work 36 (40-44) sts of right front, making buttonholes and cables of correct rows—138 (154-170) sts. Continue in pat until 9 rows beyond 5th (6th-7th) buttonhole. End on right side—about 8½ (10-11)" from underarm. **Dec Row:** Rib 6, p across to last 6 sts, dec 3 sts evenly spaced, rib 6. Change to No. 5 needles. Work in ribbing for 10 rows, making last buttonhole on 5th and 6th rows of ribbing. Bind off loosely in ribbing.

FINISHING: Steam-press lightly. Work blanket st around buttonholes. Sew on buttons.

Zippered Jacket

shown on page 101
Sizes 8, 10, 12, 14

Directions are for size 8. Changes for sizes 10, 12, and 14 are in parentheses.
COATS & CLARK'S "Red Heart Orlon Sayelle, 4 Ply" was used for the original model.

MATERIALS: Orlon Sayelle of Knitting Worsted weight—13 (14-15-17) ozs. Jacket zipper—14 (16-18-18)" long.
Knitting Needles: 1 pr each of No. 4 and No. 7 or size required to knit to gauge.

GAUGE—The Most Important Word in Knitting
5 sts = 1"; 9 rows = 1".
Detailed drawings of how to make all of the basic stitches and all abbreviations used in these directions appear in the "How-To Section"—pages 169-210.

TEST PIECE: With No. 7 needles, cast on 15 sts. Work in pat for 18 rows. Piece should measure 3 × 2 inches. If too small, try larger-size needles; if too large, try smaller-size needles until correct

Zippered Jacket instructions are on page 100.

gauge is obtained. While knitting, measure your work frequently to be sure you are maintaining the gauge.

MEASUREMENTS: At chest, closed—29½ (31-35-37)"; across back at underarms—15 (15½-17½-18½)"; across each front at underarms—7¼ (7¾-8¾-9¼)"; sleeve width at upperarm—11¾ (12½-13½-15)".

Ribbing—Row 1: K 1, * p 1, k 1; repeat from * across. **Row 2:** P 1, * k 1, p 1; repeat from * across. Repeat these 2 rows for all ribbing.

PATTERN STITCH—Multiple of 2 sts plus 1.
Row 1—wrong side: K 1, * yo, slip 1 as to p, k 1; repeat from * across. **Row 2:** K 1, * k the yo and slip st tog **through back loop of sts,** k next st through front loop of st; repeat from * across. Repeat these 2 rows for pat, taking care to keep continuity. When binding off and decreasing, always count the yo and sl st as 1 st. Accurate count of sts can be made after row 2 of pat.

BACK: With No. 4 needles, cast on 75 (79-87-93) sts. Work ribbing for 2½ (2½-3-3)". End with row 1. Change to No. 7 needles. Work
(Continued on p. 102)

even in pat until piece measures 9½ (11-12½-12½)" or desired length to underarms. End with pat row 1.
Raglan Armholes: Counting yo and sl st as 1 st, bind off 3 (3-4-4) sts at beg of next row, complete row. **Row 2:** Bind off 3 (3-4-4) sts, p 2, complete row, ending p 3. **Row 3:** K 1, sl 1, k 1, psso, work to last 3 sts, k 2 tog, k 1. **Row 4:** P 3, work pat to last 3 sts, p 3. Repeat rows 3 and 4 until 19 (19-21-21) sts remain. Bind off.

POCKET LININGS: With No. 7 needles, cast on 13 (15-15-17) sts. Work in stockinette st (k 1 row, p 1 row) for 2 (2-2½-2½)". Slip sts to a holder.

LEFT FRONT: With No. 4 needles, cast on 36 (40-44-46) sts. **Ribbing—Row 1:** K 2 (front edge), * p 1, k 1; repeat from * across. **Row 2:** P 1, * k 1, p 1; repeat from * to last 3 sts, k 3. Repeat these 2 rows for 2½ (2½-3-3)". End at front edge. Change to No. 7 needles. **Pat Row 1—wrong side:** K 2, * yo, sl 1, k 1; repeat from * across. **Row 2:** K 1, * k the yo and sl st tog **through back loops of sts,** k 1; repeat from *, ending k 2. Repeat these 2 rows until piece measures 3 (3-3½-3½)". End at side edge.
Pocket—Row 1: Work pat across 13 (13-15-15) sts, slip remaining sts to a holder; with k side of lining to you, k across 13 (15-15-17) sts of lining. **Row 2:** P 13 (15-15-17) of lining, work pat across remaining sts. **Row 3:** Work pat across 13 (13-15-15) sts, k 13 (15-15-17) sts of lining. Repeat last 2 rows for 4 (4-4½-4½)".

End with row 2. **Next Row**: Work pat across 13 (13-15-15) sts, bind off 13 (15-15-17) sts of lining. Slip sts to a holder. Attach yarn at beg of pocket opening, work pat across 23 (27-29-31) sts of front and continue until same length as opening. End at front edge. **Next Row**: Work across sts of front and across 13 (13-15-15) sts from holder—36 (40-44-46) sts. Continue in pat until same length as back to underarm. End at side edge.

Raglan Armhole and Neck Shaping: Bind off 3 (3-4-4) sts at beg of next row. On next row work to last 3 sts, p 3. **Row 3**: K 1, sl 1, k 1, psso, complete row. **Row 4**: Work to last 3 sts, p 3. Repeat last 2 rows until armhole measures 4½ (5-5½-5½)". End at front edge. Bind off 4 (5-6-6) sts at beg of next row. Continuing raglan decs, at neck edge dec 1 st every other row 4 (5-5-5) times. Work raglan decs until 2 sts remain. K 2 tog.

RIGHT FRONT: With No. 4 needles, cast on 36 (40-44-46) sts. **Ribbing—Row 1**: * K 1, p 1; repeat from * to last 2 sts, k 2 (front edge). **Row 2**: K 3, p 1, * k 1, p 1; repeat from * across. Complete ribbing same as left front, ending at side edge. Change to No. 7 needles. **Pat Row 1**: * K 1, yo, sl 1; repeat from * to last 2 sts, k 2. **Row 2**: K 2, * k the yo and sl st tog **through back loop of sts,** k 1; repeat from * across. Complete to correspond to left front, reversing all shaping and position of pocket opening. Make raglan decs same as left side of back.

SLEEVES: With No. 4 needles, cast on 43 (47-51-55) sts. Work in ribbing for 2½ (2½-3-3)". Change to No. 7 needles. Work in pat, inc 1 st each side every 8th row 8 (8-9-10) times—59 (63-69-75) sts. Work even until sleeve measures 13 (14½-16-17½)" or desired length to underarm.

Raglan Shaping: Shape same as back until 3 sts remain. Bind off.

FINISHING: Steam-press pieces lightly. Sew sleeves to fronts and back. Sew underarm and sleeve seams. Sew pocket linings in place. **Neckband**: With right side to you using No. 4 needles, pick up 67 (69-73-77) sts all around neck edge. Work 4 rows of ribbing. Dec 1 st each side *every* row until band measures 2½ (2½-3-3)" at center back. Bind off in ribbing. Fold band in half to wrong side and sew along picked-up row. If desired work 1 row sc along each front edge and around pocket openings. Sew in zipper.

Tweed Stitch Pullover

shown on page 105
Sizes 4, 6, 8, 10, 12, 14

Directions are for size 4. Changes for sizes 6, 8, 10, 12, and 14 are in parentheses.
COLUMBIA-MINERVA "Knitting Worsted" was used for the original model.

MATERIALS: Knitting Worsted—or—Nantuk Knitting Worsted—Main Color (MC)—8 (8-9-10-10-11) ozs; Colors A and B—3 (3-4-4-5-5-5) ozs of each color.
Knitting Needles: 1 pr each of No. 5 and No. 9 or size required to knit to gauge. 1 set of No. 5 dp needles.

GAUGE—The Most Important Word in Knitting
9 sts = 2″; 6 rows = 1″.
Detailed drawings of how to make all of the basic stitches and all abbreviations used in these directions appear in the "How-To Section"—pages 169-210.

TEST PIECE: With No. 9 needles and MC, cast on 19 sts. Work in pat for 24 rows. Piece should measure 4 × 4 inches. If too small, try larger-size needles; if too large, try smaller-size needles until correct gauge is obtained. While knitting, measure your work frequently to be sure you are maintaining the gauge.
(Continued on p. 106)

Tweed Stitch Pullover instructions are on page 104.

MEASUREMENTS: Chest—24 (26-28-30-32-34)"; across back or front at underarms—12 (13-14-15-16-17)"; sleeve width at upperarm—10½ (11-11½-12-12¼-12½)".

PATTERN STITCH—Uneven multiple of sts.
Row 1—right side: With B, k 1, * yarn in front, sl 1, yarn in back, k 1; repeat from * across. **Row 2**: With B, purl. **Row 3**: With A, k 1, * with yarn in back sl 1, k 1; repeat from * across. **Row 4**: With A, purl. **Row 5**: With MC, k 1, * yarn in front, sl 1, k 1; repeat from * across. **Row 6**: With MC, purl. **Rows 7-8**: With B, repeat rows 3 and 4. **Rows 9-10**: With A, repeat rows 1 and 2. **Rows 11-12**: With MC, repeat rows 3 and 4. Repeat these 12 rows for pat st and colors.

BACK: With No. 5 needles and MC, cast on 54 (58-62-66-72-76) sts. K 1, p 1 in ribbing for 2". P 1 row, inc 1 st at end of row. Change to No. 9 needles. Work even in pat until piece measures 10 (10½-11-12-12-12½)" or desired length to underarms.
Armholes: Keeping continuity of pat, bind off 2 (3-3-3-4-5) sts at beg of next 2 rows. Dec 1 st each side every other row 3 (3-4-4-5-5) times—45 (47-49-53-55-57) sts. Work even until armholes measure 3¼ (3¾-4-4¼-4¾-5)". On next p row slip center 13 (13-13-15-17-17) sts to a holder. Working on sts of one side, dec 1 st at neck edge every other row 4 times—12 (13-14-15-15-16) sts. Work even until armhole measures 4¾ (5-5¼-5¾-6½-7¼)".
Shoulder: From arm edge bind off 6 (6-7-7-7-8) sts once; bind off remaining 6 (7-7-8-8-8) sts. Attach yarn at opposite neck edge and work other side to correspond.

FRONT: Work same as back.

SLEEVES: With No. 5 needles and MC, cast on 35 (37-39-41-43-45) sts. K 1, p 1 in ribbing for 2". Change to No. 9 needles. Work in stockinette st (k 1 row, p 1 row) inc 1 st each side every 1" 6 times—47 (49-51-53-55-57) sts. Work even until sleeve measures 10 (11-11½-12-13-14)" or desired length.
Shaping: Bind off 3 (3-4-4-5-5) sts at beg of next 2 rows. Dec 1 st each side every other row until cap measures 3 (3¼-3½-3¾-4-4)" from bound-off sts. Bind off 2 sts at beg of next 4 rows. Bind off remaining sts.

FINISHING: Steam-press pieces lightly. Sew shoulder, underarm, and sleeve seams. Sew in sleeves.
Turtleneck: With right side to you, using No. 5 dp needles and MC, pick up 60 (64-68-72-76-80) sts all around neck including sts on holders. Divide sts evenly on 3 needles. K 1, p 1 in ribbing for 4¼ (4½-5-5-5½-5½)". Bind off very loosely in ribbing.

Classic Raglan Pullover

shown at left on page 110
Sizes 6-8 and 10-12

Directions are for size 6-8. Changes for size 10-12 are in parentheses.
FLEISHER'S "Casa-Laine Sport Yarn" was used for the original model.

MATERIALS: Sport Yarn or Sayelle Nantuk of Sport Yarn weight: 9 (11) ozs.
Knitting Needles: 1 pr each of No. 2 and No. 4 or size required to knit to gauge.

GAUGE—The Most Important Word in Knitting
7 sts = 1"; 9 rows = 1".
Detailed drawings of how to make all of the basic stitches and all abbreviations used in these directions appear in the "How-To Section"—pages 169-210.

TEST PIECE: With No. 4 needles, cast on 21 sts. Work in stockinette st (k 1 row, p 1 row) for 27 rows. Piece should measure 3 × 3 inches. If too small, try larger-size needles; if too large, try smaller-size needles until correct gauge is obtained. While knitting, measure your work frequently to be sure you are maintaining the gauge.

MEASUREMENTS: At chest—28 (32)"; across back and front at underarms—14 (16)"; sleeve width at upper arm—12 (13)".
(Continued on p. 108)

BACK: With No. 2 needles, cast on 98 (112) sts. K 1, p 1 in ribbing for 2½". Change to No. 4 needles. Work in stockinette st until piece measures 10 (12½)" or desired length to underarms. **Raglan Armholes:** Bind off 4 (6) sts at beg of next 2 rows. **Dec Row:** K 2, sl 1, k 1, psso, k to last 4 sts, k 2 tog, k 2. P 1 row. Repeat decs every k row 30 (33) times more–28 (32) sts. Change to No. 2 needles. K 1, p 1 in ribbing for 7 rows. Bind off loosely in ribbing.

FRONT: Work same as for back until 2 (3) raglan dec rows have been completed. End with a k row–86 (94) sts. On next p row, work 43 (47) sts and slip them to a holder, complete row.
Raglan Armhole and Neck Shaping: Continuing raglan decs every other row 29 (31) times more, at neck edge dec 1 st every 4th row 13 (15) times. Fasten off. Attach yarn at center front and work other side to correspond.

SLEEVES: With No. 2 needles, cast on 56 (62) sts. K 1, p 1 in ribbing for 2½ (3)". Inc 1 st at end of last row. Change to No. 4 needles. Work in stockinette st, inc 1 st each side every 6th row 12 (14) times–81 (91) sts. Work even until sleeve measures 13 (15)" or desired length.
Raglan Shaping: Bind off 4 (6) sts at beg of next 2 rows. Work dec rows same as for back until 11 sts remain. Bind off.

FINISHING: Steam-press pieces lightly. Sew sleeves to front.

FRONT NECKBAND: With right side to you, using No. 2 needles and starting at left sleeve, pick up 11 sts across top of sleeve; pick up 59 (65) sts along left side of neck, slip a marker on needle; pick up 59 (65) sts along right neck edge and 11 sts across top of sleeve–140 (152) sts. **Row 1—wrong side:** K 1, p 1 in ribbing to marker, slip marker; p 1, k 1 in ribbing to end of row. **Row 2:** P 1, k 1 in ribbing to 2 sts before marker, k 2 tog, slip marker, sl 1, k 1, psso, k 1, p 1 in ribbing to end of row. **Row 3:** Rib to 1 st before marker, p 1, slip marker, p 1, rib to end of row. Repeat rows 2 and 3 until there are 7 rows of ribbing. Bind off loosely.

Sew sleeves to back and neckband edges tog. Sew underarm and sleeve seams.

Girl's Sleeveless Slipon

shown at right on page 110
Sizes 4, 6, 8, 10, 12, 14

Directions are for size 4. Changes for sizes 6, 8, 10, 12, and 14 are in parentheses.
FLEISHER'S "Supra Mohair" was used for the original model.

MATERIALS: Mohair (50-gram ball): 4 (5-5-6-6-7-7) balls.
Knitting Needles: 1 pr each of No. 6 and No. 10 or size required to knit to gauge.

GAUGE—The Most Important Word in Knitting
4 sts = 1"; 5 rows = 1".
Detailed drawings of how to make all of the basic stitches and all abbreviations used in these directions appear in the "How-To Section"—pages 169-210.

TEST PIECE: With No. 10 needles, cast on 16 sts. Work in stockinette st (k 1 row, p 1 row) for 20 rows. Piece should measure 4 × 4 inches. If too small, try larger-size needles; if too large, try smaller-size needles until correct gauge is obtained. While knitting, measure your work frequently to be sure you are maintaining the gauge.

MEASUREMENTS: At chest—24 (26-28-30-32-34)"; across back and front at underarms—12 (13-14-15-16-17)".

FRONT NECK FACING: With No. 10 needles, cast on 8 sts. P 1 row, k 1 row for 8 rows. Divide sts, placing 4 sts on each of 2 holders.

FRONT: With No. 6 needles, cast on 48 (52-56-60-64-68) sts. Work in stockinette st (k 1 row, p 1 row) for 11 rows. K next row on wrong side, working into back loop of each st for turning ridge. Work even for 2". Change to No. 10 needles and continue in stockinette st until piece measures 8½ (9-9½-10½-11½-11½)" above

(Continued on p. 111)

Classic Raglan Pullover instructions are on page 107.
Girl's Sleeveless Slipon instructions are on page 109.

turning ridge or desired length to underarms. End with a p row. **Armhole and Neck:** Cast on 4 sts at beg of next row, k until there are 28 (30-32-34-36-38) sts on needle; with k side to you starting at center, k 4 sts of front facing to same needle—32 (34-36-38-40-42) sts. Slip remaining 4 sts of facing and 24 (26-28-30-32-34) sts of right front to a holder. Working on sts of one side, p 1 row. **Dec Row:** K 4, yarn in back, sl 1 as to p for turning st, k to last 10 sts, k 2 tog, k 3, yarn in back, sl 1 for turning st, k 4. P 1 row. Keeping arm edge even, repeat dec every other row 5 times; every 4th row 4 (4-4-5-5-5) times—22 (24-26-27-29-31) sts. Work even until 6 (6½-7-7-7½-7½)" above cast-on sts at underarm. End with a p row. Mark arm edge for shoulder. Work 2 more rows. On next row work to 4 sts at front edge; bind off these 4 sts. Slip remaining 18 (20-22-23-25-27) sts to a holder.

RIGHT FRONT: With right side to you, k across 4 sts of facing and 24 (26-28-30-32-34) sts of front, cast on 4 sts at end of row. P 1 row. **Dec Row:** K 4, sl 1 as to p, k 3, sl 1, k 1, psso, k to last 5 sts, sl 1, k 4. Complete to correspond to left front until 2 rows above shoulder marker. End at front edge. **Next Row:** Bind off 4 sts of front facing, k to end of row—18 (20-22-23-25-27) sts. Leave sts on needle. Do not break yarn.

BACK NECK FACING: With No. 6 needles, cast on 28 (28-28-30-30-30) sts. P 1 row, k 1 row for 4 rows. Continuing stockinette st, bind off 4 sts at beg of next 2 rows—20 (20-20-22-22-22) sts. End with a k row.

BACK: With wrong side to you, p across 18 (20-22-23-25-27) sts of right shoulder; k across 20 (20-20-22-22-22) sts of back facing for turning ridge; p 18 (20-22-23-25-27) sts of left shoulder—56 (60-64-68-72-76) sts. Continuing slip sts at each side, work even until armhole measures same as front. Bind off 4 sts at beg of next 2 rows—48 (52-56-60-64-68) sts. Complete to correspond to front.

FINISHING: Sew underarm seams. Fold facings to wrong side on slip sts and turning ridge and sew in place. Sew ends of facings tog at shoulders. Turn hem to wrong side on turning ridge and sew. Steam-press lightly.

Irish Fisherman Knit Pullover

shown on page 113
Sizes 4, 6, 8, 10, 12, 14

Directions are for size 4. Changes for sizes 6, 8, 10, 12, and 14 are in parentheses.
COATS & CLARK'S "Red Heart Knitting Worsted, 4 Ply" was used for the original model.

MATERIALS:Knitting Worsted or Sayelle Nantuk of Knitting Worsted weight—12 (14-16-18-20-22) ozs.
Knitting Needles: 1 set of No. 5 dp needles. 1 pr each of No. 5 and No. 8 or size required to knit to gauge.

GAUGE—The Most Important Word in Knitting

Center diamond panel, including 2 cables—5½" wide—24 rows of pat = 4".

Popcorn Stitch at sides and sleeves—5 popcorns = 3"; 12 rows = 2". Overall Average across a row—5 sts = 1"; 6 rows = 1".
Detailed drawings of how to make all of the basic stitches and all abbreviations used in these directions appear in the "How-To Section"—pages 169-210.

TEST PIECE—Worked in popcorn st. With No. 8 needles, cast on 22 sts. **Row 1**: Purl. **Row 2**: K 1, * k, yo and k in next st, k 3 tog; repeat from *, end k 1. **Row 3**: Purl. **Row 4**: K 1, * k 3 tog, k, yo and k in next st; repeat from *, end k 1. Repeat these 4 rows twice more. Piece should measure 4 × 2 inches. If too small, try larger-size needles; if too large, try smaller-size needles until correct gauge is obtained. While knitting, measure your work frequently to be sure you are maintaining the gauge.

MEASUREMENTS: Chest, approx.—25 (27-29-31-33-35)"; across back and front at underarms—12½ (13½-14½-15½-16½-17½)"; sleeve width at upperarm—9½ (10½-11½-12½-13½-14½)".

TWISTED RIBBING—Row 1—right side: P 1, * k in back loop of next st, p 1; repeat from * across. **Row 2**: * K in back loop of next st, p 1; repeat from * across, ending k in back loop of last st. Repeat these 2 rows for all ribbing.

(Continued on p. 114)

Irish Fisherman Knit Pullover instructions are on page 112.

PATTERN STITCH—Row 1—right side: P to marker, slip marker, k 6, p 7, k 2, p 1, k 2, p 7, k 6, slip marker, p to end of row.

Row 2: K 1, (k, yo and k in next st, k 3 tog) to marker, slip marker; p 6, k 7, p 2, k 1, p 2, k 7, p 6, slip marker; (k 3 tog, k, yo and k in next st) across, end k 1. Slip markers every row.

Row 3: P to marker, slip next 3 sts to dp needle, hold in back of work k next 3 sts, k 3 from dp needle—cable made; p 7; slip next 3 sts to dp needle, hold in back of work, k next 2 sts, slip 3rd st from dp needle back to left-hand needle, bring dp needle with 2 sts to front of work, p the st on left-hand needle, k 2 sts from dp needle, p 7; slip next 3 sts to dp needle, hold in back of work, k next 3 sts, k 3 sts from dp needle (cable made); p to end of row.

Row 4: K 1, (k 3 tog, k, yo and k in next st) to marker; p 6, k 7, p 2, k 1, p 2, k 7, p 6; (k, yo and k in next st, k 3 tog) across, end k 1. (Hereafter the abbreviation dp refers to dp needle.)

Row 5: P to marker, k 6, p 6, slip next st to dp, hold in back, k next 2 sts, p 1 from dp, p 1, slip next 2 sts to dp, hold in front, p next st, k 2 from dp, p 6, k 6, p to end of row.

Row 6: K 1, (k, yo and k in next st, k 3 tog) to marker; p 6, k 6, p 2, k 1; k, yo and k in next st; k 1, p 2, k 6, p 6; (k 3 tog, k, yo and k in next st) across, end k 1.

Row 7: P to marker, k 6, p 5, slip next st to dp, hold in back, k 2, p 1 from dp, p 5, slip 2 sts to dp, hold in front, p 1, k 2 from dp, p 5; k 6; p to end of row.

Row 8: K 1, (k 3 tog, k, yo and k in next st) to marker; p 6, k 5, p 2, k 1, k, yo and k in next st, k 3 tog, k, yo and k in next st, k 1, p 2, k 5, p 6; (k, yo and k in next st, k 3 tog) across, k 1.

Row 9: P to marker, cable over next 6 sts, p 4, slip next st to dp, hold in back, k next 2 sts, p 1 from dp, p 9, slip next 2 sts to dp, hold in front, p next st, k 2 from dp, p 4; cable over next 6 sts, p to end of row.

Row 10: K 1, (k, yo and k in next st, k 3 tog) to marker; p 6, k 4, p 2, k 1, (k, yo and k in next st, k 3 tog) twice, k, yo and k in next st, k 1, p 2, k 4, p 6; (k 3 tog, k, yo and k in next st) across, ending k 1.

Row 11: P to marker, k 6, p 3, slip next st to dp, hold in back, k next 2 sts, p 1 from dp, p 13, slip next 2 sts to dp, hold in front, p 1, k 2 from dp, p 3, k 6, p to end of row.

Row 12: K 1, (k 3 tog, k, yo and k in next st) to marker; p 6, k 3, p 2, k 1, (k, yo and k in next st, k 3 tog) 3 times, k, yo and k in next st, k 1, p 2, k 3, p 6; (k, yo and k in next st, k 3 tog), end k 1.

Row 13: P to marker, k 6, p 2, slip next st to dp, hold in back, k 2, p 1 from dp, p 17, slip next 2 sts to dp, hold in front, p 1, k 2 from dp, p 2, k 6; p to end of row.

Row 14: K 1, (k, yo and k in next st, k 3 tog) to marker; p 6, k 2, p 2, k 1, (k, yo and k in next st, k 3 tog) 4 times, k, yo and k in next st, k 1, p 2, k 2, p 6; (k 3 tog, k, yo and k in next st), end k 1.

Row 15: P to marker, cable over next 6 sts, p 2, k 2, p 21, k 2, p 2, cable over next 6 sts, p to end of row.

Pattern now starts in reverse.

Row 16: K 1, (k 3 tog, k, yo and k in next st) to marker, p 6, k 2, p 2, k 1, k 3 tog, (k, yo and k in next st, k 3 tog) 4 times; k 1, p 2, k 2, p 6, (k, yo and k in next st, k 3 tog), end k 1.

Row 17: P to marker, k 6, p 2, slip next 2 sts to dp, hold in front, p 1, k 2 from dp, p 17, slip next st to dp, hold in back, k 2, p 1 from dp, p 2, k 6; p to end of row.

Row 18: K 1, (k, yo and k in next st, k 3 tog) to marker; p 6, k 3, p 2, k 1, k 3 tog, (k, yo and k in next st, k 3 tog) 3 times; k 1, p 2, k 3, p 6, (k 3 tog, k, yo, k in next st), end k 1.

Row 19: P to marker, k 6, p 3, slip next 2 sts to dp, hold in front, p 1, k 2 from dp, p 13, slip next st to dp, hold in back, k 2, p 1 from dp, p 3, k 6; p to end of row.

Row 20: K 1, (k 3 tog, k, yo and k in next st) to marker; p 6, k 4, p 2, k 1, k 3 tog, (k, yo and k in next st, k 3 tog) twice; k 1, p 2, k 4, p 6 (k, yo and k in next st, k 3 tog) across, end k 1.

Row 21: P to marker, cable over next 6 sts, p 4, slip next 2 sts to dp, hold in front, p 1, k 2 from dp, p 9, slip next st to dp, hold in back, k 2, p 1 from dp, p 4, cable over next 6 sts, p to end.

(Continued on p. 116)

Row 22: K 1, (k, yo and k in next st, k 3 tog) to marker; p 6, k 5, p 2, k 1, k 3 tog, k, yo and k in next st, k 3 tog, k 1, p 2, k 5, p 6, (k 3 tog, k, yo and k in next st), end k 1.
Row 23: P to marker, k 6, p 5, slip next 2 sts to dp, hold in front, p 1, k 2 from dp, p 5, slip next st to dp, hold in back, k 2, p 1 from dp, p 5, k 6, p to end of row.
Row 24: K 1, (k 3 tog, k, yo and k in next st) to marker; p 6, k 6, p 2, k 1, k 3 tog, k 1, p 2, k 6, p 6, (k, yo and k in next st, k 3 tog), end k 1.
Repeat rows 1 through 24 for pattern.

BACK: With No. 5 needles, cast on 59 (67-75-83-91-99) sts. Work in twisted ribbing for 2 (2-2¼-2¼-2¾-2¾)". End with row 2. Rib next row inc 6 sts evenly spaced—65 (73-81-89-97-105) sts. **Next Row**: Rib 17 (21-25-29-33-37) sts, slip a marker on needle; rib next 31 sts; slip a marker on needle, rib remaining 17 (21-25-29-33-37) sts. Change to No. 8 needles. Starting with row 1, work even in pat until piece measures 9 (10-10½-11-12-12)" or desired length to underarms.
Armholes: Bind off 4 sts at beg of next 2 rows—57 (65-73-81-89-97) sts. Work even until armholes measure 4 (4½-4¾-5¼-6-6)" above bound-off sts. End with a row on right side.

NOTE: There are 2 extra sts in each popcorn in the diamond. These 3 sts (k, yo and k) are counted as 1 st.
Neck: Work across 20 (23-26-30-33-37) sts; work center 17 (19-21-21-23-23) sts knitting 3 sts of each popcorn tog across diamond, slip these sts to a holder; work remaining 20 (23-26-30-33-37) sts. Working on sts of one side, at neck edge bind off 2 (2-2-2-3-3) sts 1 (1-2-2-2-2) times. Dec 1 st at same edge *every* row 2 (3-3-5-5-7) times—16 (18-19-21-22-24) sts. Work even until armhole measures 5 (5½-5¾-6¼-6½-7¼)".
Shoulder: From arm edge bind off 6 (8-7-7-8-8) sts once; 5 (5-6-7-7-8) sts twice. Attach yarn at opposite neck edge and work other side to correspond.

FRONT: Work same as back. Sew shoulder seams.

SLEEVES: With right side to you, using No. 8 needles, pick up 49 (57-65-73-81-89) sts along straight edge of armhole, leaving bound-off sts free. **Row 2—wrong side**: K 1, (k, yo and k in next st, k 3 tog) 2 (3-4-5-6-7) times, slip a marker on needle; p 6, k 7, p 2, k 1, p 2, k 7, p 6; slip a marker on needle, (k 3 tog, k, yo and k in next st) 2 (3-4-5-6-7) times, end k 1. Starting with row 3, work even in pat for 4". Keeping continuity of popcorns, dec 1 st each side of next row and repeat decs every 8 (6-4-4-4-4) rows 5 (7-10-11-11-11) times more—37 (41-43-49-57-65) sts. Work even until sleeve measures 8 (9-9½-11½-13-14)" or 2 (2-2½-2½-3-3)" less than desired finished length. End with a row on right side. On next row k tog the 3 sts of each popcorn in center of diamond. Change to No. 5 needles. Work in twisted ribbing, dec 4 (6-6-8-10-12) sts on first row—33 (35-37-41-47-53) sts. Work even until sleeve measures desired length. Bind off loosely in ribbing.

NECKBAND: With No. 5 dp needles, pick up 64 (68-72-76-80-84) sts all around neck edge, including sts on holders. Work around and around in twisted ribbing for 1½". If turtle neck is desired, work until band measures 2"; reverse work so that twisted ribbing will be to outside and continue until band measures 4 (4-5-5-6-6)". Bind off loosely in twisted ribbing. Fold narrow neckband in half to wrong side and sew in place. Fold turtle neckband to right side. Sew underarm and sleeve seams. Sew bound-off sts at underarms to sides of sleeves.

Ribbed Helmet

shown on page 118
Sizes Small, Medium, Large

Directions are for small size. Changes for medium and large sizes are in parentheses.
COLUMBIA-MINERVA "Calibrette" was used for the original model.

MATERIALS: Bulky Quick Knit Yarn of Wool and Nylon 50/50—2 ozs.
Knitting Needles: 1 pr of No. 11.
(Continued on p. 118)

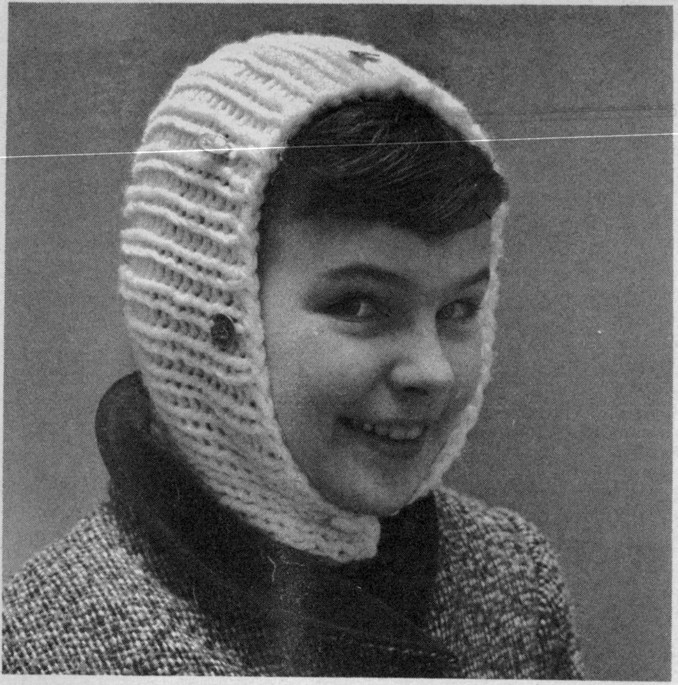

Ribbed Helmet instructions are on page 117.

GAUGE–The Most Important Word in Knitting
4 sts = 1″; 6 rows = 1″.

Detailed drawings of how to make all of the basic stitches and all abbreviations used in these directions appear in the "How-To Section"–pages 169-210.

Cast on 55 (61-67) sts. **Row 1—wrong side**: K 1, * p 1, k 1; repeat from * across. **Row 2**: P 1, * k 1, p 1; repeat from * across. Repeat rows 1, 2 and 1. **Buttonhole Row**: P 1, k 1, p 1, k 2 tog, yo, complete row. On next row work the yo as a st. Continue in ribbing until piece measures 7¼ (8-8¾)″ or desired depth. Bind off in ribbing.

Fold piece in half and sew bound-off edge tog at center back. Sew on button, trim as desired.

Mohair Cardigan

shown on page 121
Sizes 4, 6, 8, 10, 12, 14

Directions are for size 4. Changes for sizes 6, 8, 10, 12, and 14 are in parentheses.
BERNAT "Brushed Mohairspun" was used for the original model. See chart on page 210 for comparable yarns.

MATERIALS: Mohair–6 (7-8-9-10-11) ozs. 5 buttons; 2 small flower motifs for trim.
Knitting Needles: 1 pr each of No. 5 and No. 8 or size required to knit to gauge. No. 00 steel crochet hook.

GAUGE–The Most Important Word in Knitting
4 sts = 1"; 7 rows = 1".
Detailed drawings of how to make all of the basic stitches and all abbreviations used in these directions appear in the "How-To Section"– pages 169-210.

TEST PIECE: With No. 8 needles, cast on 12 sts. Work in pat for 14 rows. Piece should measure 3 × 2 inches. If too small, try larger-size needles; if too large, try smaller-size needles until correct gauge is obtained. While knitting, measure your work frequently to be sure you are maintaining the gauge.

MEASUREMENTS: At chest buttoned–25 (27-29-31-33-35)"; across back at underarms–12 (13-14-15-16-17)"; across each front at underarms–6¼ (6¾-7¼-7¾-8-8¼)"; sleeve width at upperarm–9½ (10-11-11½-12-12½)".

PATTERN STITCH–Any multiple of sts.
Row 1—right side: Knit. **Rows 2 and 3**: Purl. **Row 4**: Knit.
Repeat these 4 rows for pat.
BACK: With No. 5 needles, cast on 48 (52-56-60-64-68) sts. K 1, p 1 in ribbing for 1½ (1½-2-2-2½-2½)". Change to No. 8 needles. Work even in pat until piece measures 8½ (9-10-11-11½-12)" or desired length to underarms.
(Continued on p. 120)

Armholes: Bind off 2 (2-3-3-4-4) sts at beg of next 2 rows. Dec 1 st each side every other row 2 (3-3-4-4-5) times—40 (42-44-46-48-50) sts. Work even until armholes measure 4¾ (5-5¼-5½-6-6½)".
Shoulders: Bind off 4 (4-4-5-5-5) sts at beg of next 4 rows; 5 (6-6-5-6-6) sts at beg of next 2 rows. Bind off remaining 14 (14-16-16-16-18) sts for back of neck.

LEFT FRONT: With No. 5 needles, cast on 24 (26-28-30-32-34) sts. Work ribbing same as for back, inc 1 st at end of last row—25 (27-29-31-33-35) sts. Change to No. 8 needles. Work even in pat until same length as back to underarm. End at side edge.
Armhole: Bind off 2 (2-3-3-4-4) sts at beg of next row. Dec 1 st at same edge every other row 2 (3-3-4-4-5) times—21 (22-23-24-25-26) sts. Work even until armhole measures 2 (2¼-2½-2¾-3-3)". End at front edge.
Neck and Shoulder: Bind off 5 (5-5-5-6-6) sts at beg of next row. Dec 1 st at same edge every other row 3 (3-4-4-3-4) times—13 (14-14-15-16-16)". Work even until armhole measures same as back. End at arm edge. From arm edge bind off 4 (4-4-5-5-5) sts twice; 5 (6-6-5-6-6) sts once.

RIGHT FRONT: Work to correspond to left front, reversing all shaping.

SLEEVES: With No. 5 needles, cast on 26 (28-30-32-34-36) sts. K 1, p 1 in ribbing for 1½ (1½-2-2-2½-2½)". Change to No. 8 needles. Work in pat, inc 1 st each side every 1" 7 times—40 (42-44-46-48-50) sts. Work even until sleeve measures 10 (11-11½-12½-13½-15)" or desired length.

(Continued on p. 122)

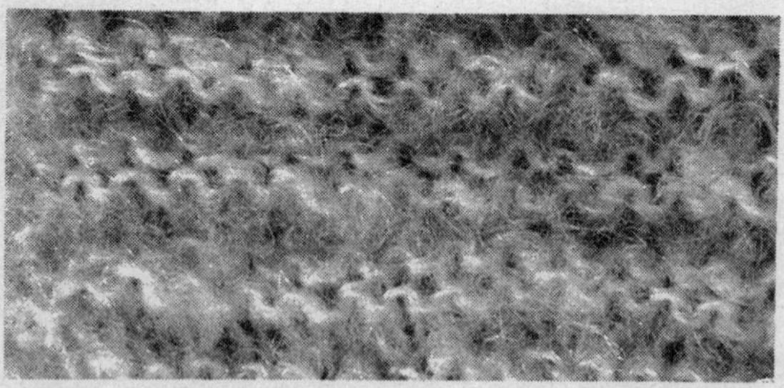

Mohair Cardigan instructions are on page 119.
Lacy Blouse and Skirt instructions are on page 122.

Shaping: Bind off 2 (2-3-3-4-4) sts at beg of next 2 rows. Dec 1 st each side every other row until cap measures 2¾ (3-3¼-3½-3½-3¾)". Bind off 2 sts at beg of next 4 rows. Bind off remaining sts.

COLLAR: With No. 5 needles, cast on 63 (65-67-69-71-73) sts. **Row 1—right side**: K 1, * p 1, k 1; repeat from * across. **Row 2**: P 1, * k 1, p 1; repeat from * across. **Row 3**: Rib 31 (32-33-34-35-36) sts, slip a marker on needle, work next st, slip another marker on needle, complete row. **Row 4**: Inc 1 st each side and before first and after 2nd marker—4 sts inc. **Row 5**: Work in ribbing. Change to No. 8 needles. Keeping continuity of ribbing, continue to inc 4 sts every other row 5 times more—87 (89-91-93-95-97) sts. Bind off loosely in ribbing.

LEFT FRONT BAND: With right side to you, work 6 rows sc along front edge. Fasten off.
Mark position of 5 buttons evenly spaced along border sts, having first marker in center of ribbing, 5th marker ½" below neck edge. Space 3 more between.

RIGHT FRONT BAND: Staring at lower edge, work 2 rows sc along front edge. **Buttonhole Row**: * Sc to marker, ch 2, skip 2 sc, sc in next sc; repeat from * 4 times more, sc to end of row. On next row, work 2 sc in each ch–2 space. Work 2 more rows of sc. Fasten off.

FINISHING: Steam-press pieces lightly. Sew shoulder, underarm, and sleeve seams. Sew in sleeves. Starting and ending at first sc rows, sew cast-on edge of collar to neck edge. Sew on buttons. Sew motifs to points of collar.

Lacy Blouse and Skirt

shown on page 121
Sizes 6, 8, 10, 12, 14

Directions are for size 6. Changes for sizes 8, 10, 12, and 14 are in parentheses.
BERNAT "Meadowspun" was used for the original model.

MATERIALS: 3 Ply Fingering Yarn—**Blouse**—4 (4-5-5-6) ozs; **Skirt**—7 (8-9-10-11) ozs.
Knitting Needles: 1 pr each of No. 2 and No. 3 or size required to knit to gauge. 1 set of No. 2 dp needles.

GAUGE—The Most Important Word in Knitting
Pat St—7 sts = 1"; 12 rows = 1".
Garter St—7 sts = 1"; 14 rows = 1".
Detailed drawings of how to make all of the basic stitches and all abbreviations used in these directions appear in the "How-To Section"—pages 169-210.

TEST PIECE: With No. 3 needles, cast on 27 sts. Work in pat for 24 rows. Piece should measure 4 × 2 inches. If too small, try larger-size needles; if too large, try smaller-size needles until correct gauge is obtained. While knitting, measure your work frequently to be sure you are maintaining the gauge.

MEASUREMENTS: Chest—26 (28-30-32-34)"; across back and front at underarms—13 (14-15-16-17)"; skirt length—11 (12-13½-14-15)".

PATTERN STITCH—Multiple of 16 sts plus 11.
Rows 1-3-5-7-9-11—Wrong side: K 13, * yo, sl 1, k 15; repeat from *, ending yo, sl 1, k 13. The yo and sl st count as 1 st on these rows.
(Continued on p. 124)

Row 2: K 3, * k 2 tog, yo, k 1, yo, sl 1, k 1, psso, k 5, k 2 tog, k 5; repeat from *, ending k 2 tog, yo, k 1, yo, sl 1, k 1, psso, k 3.
Row 4: K 2, * k 2 tog, yo, k 3, yo, sl 1, k 1, psso, k 4, k 2 tog, k 4; repeat from *, ending k 2 tog, yo, k 3, yo, sl 1, k 1, psso, k 2.
Row 6: K 1, * k 2 tog, yo, k 5, yo, sl 1, k 1, psso, k 3, k 2 tog, k 3; repeat from *, ending k 2 tog, yo, k 5, yo, sl 1, k 1, psso, k 1.
Row 8: K 2, * yo, sl 1, k 1, psso, k 3, k 2 tog, yo, k 4, k 2 tog, k 4; repeat from *, ending yo, sl 1, k 1, psso, k 3, k 2 tog, yo, k 2.
Row 10: K 3, * yo, sl 1, k 1, psso, k 1, k 2 tog, yo, k 5; k 2 tog, k 5; repeat from *, ending yo, sl 1, k 1, psso, k 1, k 2 tog, yo, k 3.
Row 12: K 4, * yo, sl 1, k 2 tog, psso, yo, k 6, k 2 tog, k 6; repeat from *, ending yo, sl 1, k 2 tog, psso, yo, k 4.
Rows 13-15-17-19-21-23: K 5, * yo, sl 1, k 15, repeat from *, ending yo, sl 1, k 5. The yo and sl st count as 1 st on these rows.
Row 14: * K 5, k 2 tog, k 5, k 2 tog, yo, k 1, yo, sl 1, k 1, psso; repeat from *, ending k 5, k 2 tog, k 5.
Row 16: K 5, * k 2 tog, k 4, k 2 tog, yo, k 3, yo, sl 1, k 1, psso, k 4; repeat from *, ending k 2 tog, k 5.
Row 18: K 5, * k 2 tog, k 3, k 2 tog, yo, k 5, yo, sl 1, k 1, psso, k 3; repeat from *, ending k 2 tog, k 5.
Row 20: K 5, * k 2 tog, k 4, yo, sl 1, k 1, psso, k 3, k 2 tog, yo, k 4; repeat from *, ending k 2 tog, k 5.
Row 22: K 5, * k 2 tog, k 5, yo, sl 1, k 1, psso, k 1, k 2 tog, yo, k 5; repeat from *, ending k 2 tog, k 5.
Row 24: K 5, * k 2 tog, k 6, yo, sl 1, k 2 tog, psso, yo, k 6; repeat from *, ending k 2 tog, k 5.
Repeat these 24 rows for pat.

BLOUSE

BACK: With No. 2 needles, cast on 92 (98-104-112-118) sts. K 1, p 1 in ribbing for 2", inc 1 st at end of last row—93 (99-105-113-119) sts. Change to No. 3 needles. **Pat Row 1**: K 1 (4-7-3-6) sts, slip a marker on needle; work row 1 of pat across 91 (91-91-107-107) sts; slip a marker on needles, k 1 (4-7-3-6) sts. **Row 2**: K to marker and slip; work row 2 of pat to next marker; slip marker, k remaining sts. Keeping 91 (91-91-107-107) sts between markers in pat and remaining sts in garter st (k every row) work even until piece measures 9 (10-11-11½-12-12)" or desired length to underarms. Mark each end of last row. Continue in pat until 5¾ (5¾-6-6½-6½)" above marked row.

Shoulders: Bind off 27 (29-31-33-35) sts at beg of next 2 rows. Slip remaining 39 (41-43-47-49) sts to a holder.

FRONT: Work same as back until 3¾ (4-4¼-4½-4¾-5)" above marked row.

Neck and Shoulders: Work across 27 (29-31-33-35) sts and slip them to a holder; k across center 39 (41-43-47-49) sts, working the yo and sl sts tog as 1 st, slip these sts to a holder; complete row. Work on sts of one side until armhole measures same as back. From arm edge bind off all sts. Attach yarn at opposite neck edge and work other side to correspond.

Seam shoulders matching pats.

NECKBAND: With right side to you, using No. 2 dp needles, pick up 88 (92-96-100-104-118) sts all around neck including sts on holders. Divide sts onto 3 needles. Work around and around in k 1, p 1 ribbing for 1". Bind off in ribbing.

SLEEVEBANDS: With right side to you, using No. 2 needles, pick up 80 (84-88-92-96) sts along arm edge between marked rows. K 1, p 1 in ribbing for 1". Bind off in ribbing.

FINISHING: Sew underarm seams. Steam-press lightly.

SKIRT

Make front and back the same.

With No. 3 needles, cast on 194 (194-210-210-210) sts. **Row 1:** K 1, * k 15, yo, sl 1 as to p; repeat from *, ending k 1. **Row 2:** K 1, * k the yo and sl st tog, k 4, yo, sl 1, k 10: repeat from *, ending k 1. **Row 3:** K 1, * k 10, k the yo and sl st tog, k 4, yo, sl 1, repeat from *, ending k 1. Repeat rows 2 and 3 until piece measures 11 (12-13½-14-15)" or desired length. Bind off working the yo and sl st tog as 1 st.

Belt: With No. 3 needles, cast on 10 sts. Work in garter st until band, when stretched slightly, is 1" longer than desired waist size.

FINISHING: Seam sides of skirt, leaving 3" opening at upper left side. Sew long edge of belt to upper edge of skirt, forming pleats and allowing for 1" overlap. Fold belt and sew other edge to skirt. Run elastic through belt, fasten securely. Close with hooks and eyes.

Ski Sets for Him and Her instructions are on page 127.

Ski Sets for Him and Her

shown on page 126
Sizes 6, 8, 10, 12, 14

Directions are for size 6. Changes for sizes 8, 10, 12, and 14 are in parentheses.
COATS & CLARK'S "Red Heart Knitting Worsted, 4 Ply" was used for the original models.

MATERIALS: Knitting Worsted—White (MC)—12 (13-14-16-18) ozs; Yellow (A)—4 (4-6-8-8) ozs; Wood Brown (B)—4 (4-6-8-8) ozs; Green (C)—2 (2-3-3-4) ozs for sweater and 1 cap.
Knitting Needles: 1 pr each of No. 5 and No. 8 or size required to knit to gauge.

GAUGE—The Most Important Word in Knitting
5 sts = 1"; 13 rows = 2".
Detailed drawings of how to make all of the basic stitches and all abbreviations used in these directions appear in the "How-To Section"—pages 169-210.

TEST PIECE: With No. 8 needles, cast on 15 sts. Work in stockinette st (k 1 row, p 1 row) for 20 rows. Piece should measure 3 × 3 inches. If too small, try larger-size needles; if too large, try smaller-size needles until correct gauge is obtained. While knitting, measure work frequently to be sure you maintain the gauge.

MEASUREMENTS: At chest—25 (28-30-32¼-35)"; across back and front at underarms—12½ (14-15-16¼-17½)"; sleeve width at upper-arm—9 (10-11-12-13¼)".

Note: Always bring the color to be used from under and around the color just dropped; this twists yarns and prevents a hole in work. Use individual ½ yd strands of Color A when working borders; this will avoid carrying 3 strands across back of work. Cut colors at end of rows when working body design and start again at beg of rows where necessary.

(Continued on p. 128)

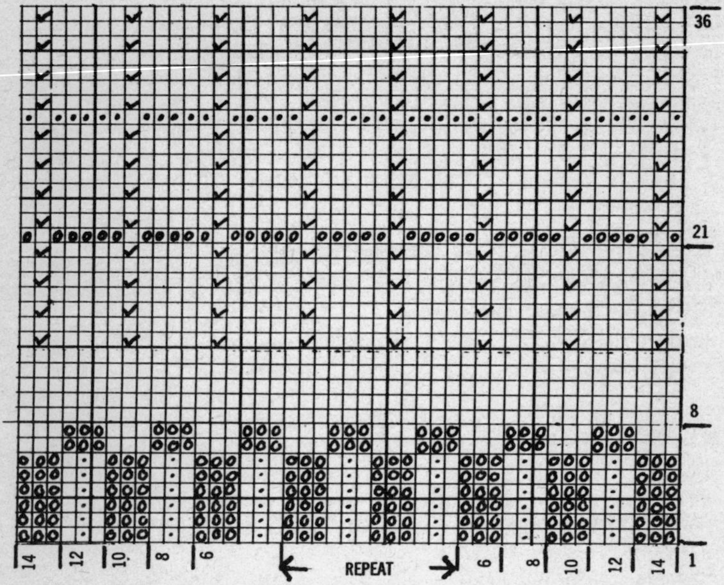

□ = MC; • = A; O = B; ✓ = C

BACK: With No. 5 needles and B, cast on 63 (69-75-81-87) sts. **Ribbing—Row 1—right side:** P 1, * k 1, p 1; repeat from * across. **Row 2:** K 1, * p 1, k 1; repeat from * across. Repeat these 2 rows 1 (1-2-2-2) times. With MC, k 1 row. Starting with row 2, work 3 (3-5-5-5) rows of ribbing. With A, k 1 row, p 1 row. Starting at size indicated, work row 1 of chart across. Read chart from right to left on k rows and from left to right on p rows, working sts between "repeat." Repeat rows 21 through 36 for body pat. Work even until piece measures 10 (11-12-13-14)" or desired length to underarms.

Armholes: Keeping continuity of design, bind off 2 (3-4-5-6) sts at beg of next 2 rows. Dec 1 st each side every other row 2 (3-4-5-5) times, discontinuing design on pat row 28 or 36. With MC, work even for 5 rows. End with a p row.

Yoke: Turn chart upside down. Centering B sts between C stripes, work rows 8 through 1. Work 2 rows of A. With B, work 6 rows ending with a p row, dec 1 st at end of last row—54 (56-58-60-64) sts. **Next Row**: K 2 B, k 2 A across row. On next row p back in colors as established. **Next 2 Rows**: K 2 A, k 2 B across row. Purl back in colors. Break off A. Continue with B until armholes measure 5 (5½-6-6½-7)".
Shoulders: Bind off 6 sts at beg of next 4 rows; 6 (7-7-8-9) sts at beg of next 2 rows. Bind off remaining 18 (18-20-20-22) sts.

FRONT: Work same as back until armholes measure 3½ (4-4-4½-5)". On last p row slip center 10 sts to a holder. Working on sts of one side and completing yoke pat, dec 1 st at neck edge every other row 4 (4-5-5-6) times—18 (19-19-20-21) sts. Work even until armhole measures same as back. From arm edge bind off 6 sts twice; 6 (7-7-8-9) sts once. Attach yarn at opposite neck edge and work other side to correspond.

SLEEVES: With B, cast on 38 (42-44-46-48) sts. K 1, p 1 in ribbing for 4 (4-6-6-6) rows. K 1 row A then rib 3 (3-5-5-5) rows. K 1 row MC, then rib 3 (3-5-5-5) rows. With B, k next row inc 2 (4-8-10-12) sts evenly spaced—40 (46-52-56-60) sts. Starting with a p row, work 5 rows stockinette st; with A, work 6 rows inc 5 (5-5-7-9) sts on last row—45 (51-57-63-69) sts. End with a p row.
Border Design: Work row 1 of chart across, starting all sizes as for size 14. Continue following chart, repeating rows 20 through 36 until sleeve measures 12 (13-14-15-16)" or desired length.
Shaping: Keeping continuity of design, bind off 2 (3-4-5-6) sts at beg of next 2 rows. Dec 1 st each side every other row until 33 sts remain. Bind off 2 sts at beg of next 8 rows. Bind off remaining sts.

FINISHING: Finish off all ends neatly. Steam-press pieces lightly. Sew right shoulder, underarm and sleeve seams.
Neckband: With right side to you, using No. 5 needles and B, pick up 68 (72-79-84-88) sts all around neck edge, including sts on holder. K 1, p 1 in ribbing for 2½ (2½-3-3½-3½)". Bind off loosely in ribbing. Seam left shoulder and neckband. Sew in sleeves. Fold collar to outside.

(Continued on p. 130)

PIGTAIL CAP

Head Sizes 18½ (20-21½)"

With No. 5 needles and B, cast on 92 (98-104) sts. K 1, p 1 in ribbing for 4 rows. With A, k 1 row, rib 3 rows. Inc 1 st at end of last row—93 (99-109) sts. Change to No. 8 needles. With A, k 1 row, p 1 row. **Design**: Starting with row 1 of chart at size 14, work even in design until piece measures 9" or desired depth. With MC only, k 2 tog across row; p 2 tog across next row. Break yarn leaving 20" end. Draw end through sts loosely. Steam-press lightly. Finish off all ends.

Braid: Cut 15 strands of A each about 1½" yds long. Tie at one end. Braid strands to desired length. Tie about 1½" from end. Trim evenly. Attach starting end of braid inside center top of cap, pulling stitches and loose end tightly around, fasten securely. Sew back seam.

BOY'S CAP

Head Sizes 18½ (20-21½)"

With No. 5 needles and A, cast on 92 (98-104) sts. K 1, p 1 in ribbing for 2½ (2½-3-3-3)", inc 1 st at end of last row—93 (99-105) sts. Change to No. 8 needles. Turn chart upside down and starting at size 14 for all sizes work rows 8 through 1 of chart. Continue in stockinette st, working 4 rows A and 4 rows B. Work rows 20 through 36 of chart until cap measures 6 (6½-7)" from center of ribbing. With MC, k 2 tog across row. P 2 tog across next row. Break yarn. Draw end through sts, pull up tight and fasten. Sew back seam. Steam-press lightly. Fold ribbing in half to wrong side and sew in place. Trim with pompon using MC, A and B.

Mohair Trimmed Knitted Cap

shown on page 131
Sizes Small, Medium, Large

Directions are for small size. Changes for medium and large sizes are in parentheses.

COLUMBIA-MINERVA "Calibrette" and "Roma" were used for the original model.

(Continued on p. 132)

Mohair Trimmed Knitted Cap instructions are on page 130.

MATERIALS: Bulky Quick Knit Yarn of Wool and Nylon 50/50—2 (2-3) ozs. Mohair—1 oz.
Knitting Needles: 1 pr of No. 11 or size required to knit to gauge. Size F crochet hook.

GAUGE—The Most Important Word in Knitting
3 sts = 1″; 4 rows = 1″.
Cast on 9 (7-8) sts. K 1 row. **Row 2:** K, inc 1 st in each st across. **Row 3:** Purl. **Row 4:** * K 1, inc in next st; repeat from * across—27 (21-24) sts. **Row 5:** Purl. **Row 6:** * K 2, inc in next st; repeat from * across—36 (28-32) sts. P 1 row. **Row 8:** * K 3, inc in next st; repeat from * across—45 (35-40) sts. Purl 1 row. Continue in this manner, inc 9 (7-8) sts every k row until there are 54 (56-64) sts. On next k row inc 2 (4-2) sts—56 (60-66) sts. Work even in stockinette st (k 1 row, p 1 row) until 3½ (4½-5¼)″ from last inc row or desired depth. Bind off on a k row. Starting at bound-off edge seam back with flat overcast sts. Do not sew cast-on edge tog.

TRIM: With right side to you using crochet hook and Mohair and starting at center back, work 1 sc around 1 knit st just below bound-off edge. Keeping working strand to right side of cap, sc around each k st around, holding in sts if necessary to control headsize—56 (60-66) sc. Ch 5, turn. **Row 2:** * Skip 3 sc, sc in 2 loops of next sc, ch 5; repeat from * around, ending ch 5. **Rnds 3 and 4:** * Sc in center of next lp, ch 5; repeat from * around, ending ch 5, sc in last loop, sl st to next sc, fasten off.
Cut as many strands of Mohair each 40 (46-50)″ long as there are loops around cap. Fold 1 strand in half, fold again and pass last folded end through any ch-5 loop, pass ends of strand through this loop and pull up evenly. Work 1 fringe in each ch-5 loop around. Thread 4 strands of 1 fringe through tapestry needle and pass needle through the purl st at top of cap—free ends of fringe are on right side at top of cap. Work all fringe evenly into the purl row at top in same manner. With wrong side to you draw opening at top of cap tog. Wrap a 12″ piece of wool tightly around all strands at top of cap, knot and finish with a small bow at center front. Trim ends of fringe evenly to desired length.

Jumbo-Knit Pullover

shown on page 135
Sizes 4, 6, 8, 10, 12, 14

Directions are for size 4. Changes for sizes 6, 8, 10, 12, and 14 are in parentheses.
COATS & CLARK'S "Red Heart Turbo-Knit" was used for the original model.

MATERIALS: Bulky Nylon and Wool—14 (16-16-18-20-24) ozs.
Knitting Needles: 1 pr each of No. 8 and No. 11 or size required to knit to gauge.

GAUGE—The Most Important Word in Knitting
3 sts = 1"; 4 rows = 1".
Detailed drawings of how to make all of the basic stitches and all abbreviations used in these directions appear in the "How-To Section"—pages 169-210.

TEST PIECE: With No. 11 needles, cast on 13 sts. Work in pat for 16 rows. Piece should measure 4 × 4 inches. If too small, try larger-size needles; if too large, try smaller-size needles until correct gauge is obtained. White knitting, measure your work frequently to be sure you are maintaining the gauge.

MEASUREMENTS: Chest—25 (27-29-31-33-35)"; across back and front at underarms—12½ (13½-14½-15½-16½-17½)"; sleeve width at upperarm—10 (11-11½-12-13-14)".

(Continued on p. 134)

PATTERN STITCH—Multiple of 4 sts plus 1.

Row 1—wrong side: Purl. **Row 2**: K 1, * yarn to front of needle, slip next 3 sts as to p, being careful to hold yarn loosely in front of the 3 slipped sts, pass yarn to back, k 1; repeat from * across. **Row 3**: Purl. **Rows 4 and 5**: Repeat rows 2 and 3. **Row 6**: K 2, * insert needle under the 2 loose strands of previous rows and k the next st, k 3; repeat from * across ending k 2 instead of k 3. **Row 7**: Purl. **Row 8**: K 3, * yarn forward, slip next 3 sts, yarn in back, k 1; repeat from *, ending last repeat k 3 instead of k 1. **Row 9**: Purl. **Rows 10 and 11**: Repeat rows 8 and 9. **Row 12**: K 4, * insert needle under the 2 loose strands of previous rows and k the next st, k 3; repeat from * across, ending last repeat k 4 instead of k 3. Repeat rows 1 through 12 for pattern.

Note: Sizes 8 and 10 only—On each knit row there is **1 more knit** st at each end of row than given in the pattern st.

BACK: With No. 8 needles, cast on 36 (40-42-46-48-52) sts. K 1, p 1 in ribbing for 2 (2½-2½-3-3-3)". On last row inc 1 st at end row—37 (41-43-47-49-53) sts. Change to No. 11 needles. Work even in pat until piece measures 9 (10-11-12-13-14)" or desired length to underarms. **Note**: If unable to complete a butterfly st before binding off or decreasing, catch loose strands, if any, on any row of pat or omit on preceding row.

Raglan Armhole: Keeping continuity of pat, bind off 2 sts at beg of next 2 rows. **Dec Row**: K 1, k 2 tog, work across to last 3 sts, k 2 tog, k 1. P 1 row. Repeat last 2 rows 9 (10-11-12-13-14) times more—13 (15-15-17-17-19) sts. Work even if necessary to end with row 1 or 7. Slip sts to a holder.

FRONT: Work same as for back until 19 (21-21-23-23-25) sts remain. End with a k row.

Neck: P across, slipping center 9 (11-11-13-13-15) sts to a holder. Working on sts of one side, continue raglan decs and dec 1 st at neck edge every other row until 2 sts remain. K 2 tog. Attach yarn at opposite neck and complete to correspond.

SLEEVES: With No. 8 needles, cast on 20 (20-22-22-24-24) sts. K 1, p 1 in ribbing for 2 (2½-2½-3-3-3½)". On last row inc 1 st. Change to No. 11 needles. Work in pat for 6 rows. Working new sts in pat, inc 1 st each side of next row and repeat incs every 6th row 4 (5-5-6-6-7) times—31 (33-35-37-39-41) sts. Work even until sleeve measures 11 (12-13-14-15-16)" or desired length.

(Continued on p. 136)

Jumbo Knit Pullover instructions are on page 133.

Raglan Shaping: Bind off 2 sts at beg of next 2 rows. Work raglan shaping same as for back until 7 sts remain. Slip sts to a holder.

FINISHING: Steam-press pieces lightly. Sew right sleeve to front and back. Sew left sleeve to front only.
Neckband: With right side to you, using No. 8 needles, k across 7 sts of left sleeve, pick up 6 sts along side of neck; k across sts of front; pick up 6 sts along other side of neck; k 7 sleeve sts; k across sts of back of neck- 48 (52-52-56-56-60) sts. K 1, p 1 in ribbing for 1 (1-1½-1½-1¾-1¾)". Bind off loosely in ribbing. Sew left sleeve to back and neckband edges tog. Sew underarm and sleeve seams.

Three Colored Pullover

shown at left on page 137
Sizes 6-8 and 10-12

Directions are for size 6-8. Changes for size 10-12 are in parentheses.
BEAR BRAND "DeLuxe Knitting Worsted" was used for the original model.

MATERIAL: Knitting Worsted—or—Nylon and Wool of Knitting Worsted weight—Color A—8 (8) ozs; Colors B and C—4 ozs of each.
Knitting Needles: 1 pr each of No. 6 and No. 8 or size required to knit to gauge.

GAUGE—The Most Important Word in Knitting
9 sts = 2"; 13 rows = 2".
Detailed drawings of how to make all of the basic stitches and all abbreviations used in these directions appear in the "How-To Section"—pages 169-210.

TEST PIECE: With No. 9 needles and A, cast on 18 sts. Work in stockinette st (k 1 row, p 1 row) for 26 rows. Piece should measure 4 × 4 inches. If too small, try larger-size needles; if too
(Continued on p. 138)

Three Colored Pullover instructions are on page 136.
Bulky Raglan Pullover instructions are on page 139.

large, try smaller-size needles until correct gauge is obtained. While knitting, measure your work frequently to be sure you are maintaining the gauge.

MEASUREMENTS: Chest—29 (32)"; across back and front at underarms—14½ (16)"; sleeve width at upperarm—11½ (13)".

BACK: With No. 6 needles and A, cast on 65 (73) sts. P 1 row, k 1 row for 10 rows. K next row on wrong side, working into back loop of each st for turning ridge. Change to No. 8 needles and continue in stockinette st until 35 (47) rows above turning ridge. End with a k row.

First Stripe: With A, p 32 (36); attach B, p 1; with another ball of A, p 32 (36). **Row 2:** With A, k 31 (35); with B, k 3; with A, k 31 (35). **Row 3:** With A, p 30 (34); with B, p 5; with A, p 30 (34). Continue in this manner, working 1 less A st each side and 2 more B sts in center until there are 27 B sts. End with a k row.

2nd Stripe: With A, p 18 (22); with B, p 14; attach C, p 1; attach another ball of B, p 14; with A, p 18 (22). **Next Row:** K 17 (21) A; 14 B; 3 C; 14 B; 17 (21) A. Continue in this manner, working 2 sts more with C at center and 1 st less with A at each side and shifting the 14 B sts of each side toward outer edges every row until there are 27 C sts. End with a k row.

3rd Stripe: Purl 4 (8) A; 14 B; 14 C; attach another ball of B, p 1; attach another ball of C, p 14; p 14 B and 4 (8) A. Continue shifting colors 1 st each row toward outer edge until 72 (84) rows above turning ridge or desired length to underarms. Mark each end of last row for underarms. End with a p row.

4th Stripe: While working raglan decs, start 4th stripe with C when there are 27 B sts at center and complete pullover with C.

Raglan Armholes—Dec Row: K 1, k 2 tog, work to last 3 sts, k 2 tog, k 1. P 1 row. Repeat decs every other row 22 (24) times—19 (23) sts. End with a k row.

Neck Facing: Change to No. 6 needles. K next row on wrong side, working into back loop of each st for turning ridge. Continue in stockinette st, inc 1 st each side every k row 3 (4) times—25 (31) sts. Bind off.

FRONT: Work same as back.

SLEEVES: With No. 6 needles and A, cast on 36 (40) sts. K 1, p 1 in ribbing for 20 rows. Inc 3 sts evenly spaced on last row—39 (43) sts. Change to No. 8 needles. Work in stockinette st, inc 1 st each side every 8th row 5 times—49 (53) sts. Work even until 41 (47) rows above ribbing. End with a k row.
First Stripe: With A, p 24 (26); attach B, p 1; attach another ball of A, p 24 (26). Working stripes same as back, continue to inc 1 st each side every 8th row until there are 51 (59) sts. Work to same pat row as back at underarms. Mark each end of last row.
Raglan Shaping: Work dec row same as for back, keeping continuity of stripes until 5 (9) sts remain. End with a k row. Change to No. 6 needles. K next row on wrong side in back loop of sts for turning ridge and continue in stockinette st, inc 1 st each side every other row 3 (4) times—11 (17) sts. Bind off.

FINISHING: Steam-press pieces lightly. Sew sleeves to front and back, matching colors. Sew facing edges tog. Turn facings to wrong side and hem. Sew underarm and sleeve seams.

Bulky Raglan Pullover

shown at right on page 137
Sizes 4-6, 8-10, 12-14

Directions are for size 4-6. Changes for sizes 8-10 and 12-14 are in parentheses.
FLEISHER'S "Nubby Fleece" was used for the original model.

MATERIALS: Extra Bulky Yarn: 18 (20-22) ozs.
Knitting Needles: 1 pr each of No. 10 and No. 13 or size required to knit to gauge.

GAUGE—The Most Important Word in Knitting
11 sts = 4"; 4 rows = 1".
Detailed drawings of how to make all of the basic stitches and all abbreviations used in these directions appear in the "How-To Section"—pages 169-210.
(Continued on p. 140)

TEST PIECE: With No. 13 needles, cast on 11 sts. Work in stockinette st for 16 rows. Piece should measure 4 × 4 inches. If too small, try larger-size needles; if too large, try smaller-size needles until correct gauge is obtained. While knitting, measure your work frequently to be sure you are maintaining the gauge.

MEASUREMENTS: At chest—28 (32-36)"; across back and front at underarms—14 (16-18)"; sleeve width at upperarm—13 (14-15)".

BACK: Starting at neck facing using No. 10 needles, cast on 18 (20-22) sts. P 1 row. **Dec Row:** K 2, sl 1, k 1, psso, k to last 4 sts, k 2 tog, k 2. Repeat these 2 rows twice more—12 (14-16) sts. P 1 row, k 1 row. K next row on wrong side, working into back loop of each st for turning ridge. K 1 row. Change to No. 13 needles, p 1 row.

Raglan Shaping: K 2, inc in next st, k to last 3 sts, inc in next st, k 2. P 1 row. Repeat these 2 rows 12 (14-16) times—38 (44-50) sts. Mark each end of last row for underarms.

Body: Continue in stockinette st until 7½ (9½-11)" from marked row. Dec 2 (0-2) sts across last row—36 (44-48) sts. Change to No. 10 needles. K 2, p 2 in ribbing for 2 (3-3)". Bind off loosely in ribbing.

FRONT: Work same as for back.

SLEEVES: Starting at neck facing using No. 10 needles, cast on 16 (14-14) sts. Work facing and turning ridge same as for back—10 (8-8) sts. Change to No. 13 needles. Work raglan shaping same as for back until there are 36 (38-42) sts. Mark each end of last row. Continue in stockinette st for 1½ (2-2)". End with a p row. **Dec Row:** K 1, sl 1, k 1, psso, k to last 3 sts, k 2 tog, k 1. Repeat decs every 1½ (2-2)" 3 (3-4) times more—28 (30-32) sts. Work even until 8 (10-12)" from marked row or until 2 (3-3)" less than desired sleeve length. On last row dec 8 (6-8) sts evenly spaced—20 (24-24) sts. Change to No. 10 needles. K 2, p 2 in ribbing for 2 (3-3)". Bind off loosely in ribbing.

FINISHING: Steam-press pieces lightly. Sew sleeves to front and back. Sew ends of facings tog. Turn facings to wrong side on turning ridges and sew in place. Sew underarm and sleeve seams. Sew on school letter if desired.

Hood-Coat and Mittens

shown at left on page 143
Sizes 6-8 and 10-12

Directions are for size 6-8. Changes for size 10-12 are in parentheses.
BEAR BRAND "Nubby Fleece" and BUCILLA "Angora" were used for the original model.

MATERIALS: Extra Bulky Yarn—26 (30) ozs. Angora—2 balls. 1 separating zipper.
Knitting Needles: 1 pr each of No. 10½ and No. 13 or size required to knit to gauge. Plastic crochet hook Size H (6).

GAUGE—The Most Important Word in Knitting
11 sts = 4"; 4 rows = 1".
Detailed drawings of how to make all of the basic stitches and all abbreviations used in these directions appear in the "How-To Section"—pages 169-210.

TEST PIECE: With No. 13 needles, cast on 11 sts. Work in stockinette st (k 1 row, p 1 row) for 12 rows. Piece should measure 4 × 3 inches. If too small, try larger-size needles; if too large, try smaller-size needles until correct gauge is obtained. While knitting, measure work frequently to be sure you maintain the gauge.

MEASUREMENTS: At chest, closed—30½ (34½)"; across back at underarms—15 (17)"; sleeve width at upperarm—12 (13)".

HOOD: Starting at top of hood, with No. 13 needles, cast on 5 sts. **Row 1**: Purl. **Row 2**: K 1, inc in each of next 2 sts, k 2—7 sts. **Row 3 and all odd rows**: Purl. **Row 4—right side**: Inc in each of first 2 sts, k 2, inc in each of next 2 sts, k 1—11 sts. **Row 6**: K 1, inc in each of next 2 sts, k 4, inc in each of next 2 sts, k to end of row—15 sts. **Row 7**: P 4, slip a marker on needle, p to last 3 sts, slip another marker on needle, p 3. **Row 8**: K to within 1 st of marker, * inc in next st, slip marker, inc in next st *, k
(Continued on p. 142)

to within 1 st of next marker, repeat between *'s once, k to end of row—19 sts. **Row 9:** P, slipping markers. Repeat last 2 rows 15 (17) times. Repeat row 8 once more. End with a k row—83 (91) sts. **Dividing Row:** Removing markers, p 20 (22), slip these sts to a holder; bind off next 43 (47) sts for front of hood; p 20 (22); p across 20 (22) sts on holder. Sew seam at center back of hood.

COAT: Neck Shaping—Row 1: With No. 10½ needles, cast on 9 sts for front border and facing sts. K the 9 cast-on sts, k next 10 (12) sts; k 2 tog 10 times; k 10 (12), cast on 9 sts for front and facing—48 (52) sts. **Row 2:** P. **Row 3:** K 5, slip next st for turning st, k to last 6 sts, slip 1, k 5. Repeat rows 2 and 3, 3 times more. **Row 10:** P 13 (14) for right front, slip a marker on needle; p 5 for sleeve; slip a marker on needle, p 13 (15) for back, slip a marker on needle; p 5 for sleeve; slip a marker on needle, p 12 (13) for left front. Carry markers and slip them every row.
Raglan Shaping—Row 1: With No. 13 needles, k 5, sl 1, * k to within 1 st of marker, inc in next st, sl marker, inc in next st; repeat from * 3 times more, k to last 6 sts, sl 1, k 5—56 (60) sts. **Row 2:** P, slipping markers. Repeat rows 1 and 2, 13 (14) times—160 (172) sts. End with a k row. Discard markers. **Dividing Row:** P 27 (29), slip these sts to a holder for right front; p 32 (34) for sleeve, slip sts to a holder; p 42 (46) for back, slip sts to a holder; p 32 (34) for left sleeve; slip remaining 27 (29) sts to a holder.

LEFT SLEEVE: Work in stockinette st, casting on 1 st at beg of next 2 rows for size 10-12 only—32 (36) sts. Work even in stockinette st for 2". **Dec Row:** K 1, sl 1, k 1, psso, k to last 3 sts, k 2 tog, k 1. Repeat decs every 2½" 3 (4) times—24 (26) sts. Work even until 12 (14)" from dividing row. End with a k row. Change to No. 10½ needles. K next row on wrong side for turning ridge and continue for 2" for facing. Bind off. Attach yarn and work right sleeve to correspond.

POCKET FACINGS: With No. 10½ needles, cast on 10 sts. Work in stockinette st for 1". End with a k row. Slip sts to holder.

BODY: With wrong side to you, using No. 13 needles, p across 27 (29) sts of left front. **Next Row:** Continuing sl sts, work 27 (29) sts of left front; cast on 0 (2) sts; k 42 (46) sts of back; cast on
(Continued on p. 144)

Hood-Coat and Mittens instructions are on page 141.
School Coat instructions are on page 145.

0 (2) sts, work 27 (29) sts of right front—96 (108) sts. P 1 row and continue until 5½ (7½)" from dividing row. End with a p row. **Pocket Openings**: Work 26 (28) sts, place last 10 sts on holder; k 54 (62), place last 10 sts on a holder; complete row. **Next Row**: P 16 (18); * with p side to you, k across 10 sts of pocket facing for turning ridge *, p 44 (52) sts; repeat between *'s once, p to end of row—96 (108) sts. Work even until 11 (13)" from underarm or desired length. End with a k row. **Next Row**: Change to No. 10½ needles, bind off 11 sts as to p for front facing; k to last 11 sts, bind off 11 sts as to p. Attach yarn on right side and continue for 2" for hem. Bind off.

POCKET LINING: With No. 13 needles, work across sts of pocket lining, and continue for 12 rows. Bind off.

FINISHING: Sew sleeve seams. Turn front, lower edge, sleeve, and pocket facings to wrong side on turning ridges or sl sts and hem. Sew pocket linings to wrong side. With right side to you work 1 row of sc on front of hood. Steam-press lightly. Sew zipper to front edges. With MC make a small pompon for zipper. With Angora make 7, 2" pompons and sew to front of hood as pictured.

MITTENS

With No. 10½ needles, cast on 20 sts. K 1, p 1 in ribbing for 9 (11) rows. Inc 1 st at end of last row—21 sts. K 1 row, p 1 row. **Thumb Gore and Thumb**: K 9, inc in next st, k 1, inc in next st, k 9—23 sts. P 1 row. **2nd Inc Row**: K 9, inc in next st, k 3, inc in next st, k 9—25 sts. P 1 row. **3rd Inc Row**: K 9, inc, k 5, inc, k 9. P 1 row. **4th Inc Row**: K 9, inc, k 7, inc, k 9. P 1 row. **Next Row**: K 10, slip these sts to a holder, k next 9 sts for thumb; slip last 10 sts to a holder. Work even on thumb sts for 1¼ (1½)". K 2 tog across row—5 sts. Break yarn, draw end through sts, pull up tight and fasten; sew thumb seam.
Hand: Attach yarn at thumb seam, k across 10 sts. P across all 20 sts, thus joining and continue in stockinette st for 2 (2½)". End with a p row. **Dec Row 1**: * K 2, k 2 tog; repeat from * across. P 1 row. **Dec Row 2**: * K 1, k 2 tog; repeat from * across—10 sts. P 1 row. Break yarn and complete as for thumb. Make other mitten the same.

School Coat

shown at right on page 143
Sizes 4-6, 8-10, 12-14

Directions are for size 4-6. Changes for sizes 8-10 and 12-14 are in parentheses.
FLEISHER'S "Big Spice" was used for the original model.

MATERIALS: Extra-Bulky Yarn—24 (28-32) ozs. 4 buttons.
Knitting Needles: 1 pr of No. 10½. 1 Circular or pr of Jumper Needles No. 13 or size required to knit to gauge. Plastic crochet hook Size J (9).

GAUGE—The Most Important Word in Knitting
11 sts = 4"; 17 rows = 4".
Detailed drawings of how to make all of the basic stitches and all abbreviations used in these directions appear in the "How-To Section"—pages 169-210.
(Continued on p. 146)

TEST PIECE: With No. 13 needles, cast on 11 sts. Work in pat for 17 rows. Piece should measure 4 × 4 inches. If too small, try larger-size needles; if too large, try smaller-size needles until correct gauge is obtained. While knitting, measure your work frequently to be sure you are maintaining the gauge.

MEASUREMENTS: At chest, buttoned—30 (34-38)"; across back at underarms—15 (17-18½)"; sleeve width at upperarm—12 (13½-15)".

PATTERN STITCH—Uneven multiple of sts.
Row 1—right side: Knit. **Row 2:** P 1, * k 1, p 1; repeat from * across. **Row 3:** Knit. **Row 4:** K 1, * p 1, k 1; repeat from * across. Repeat these 4 rows for pat st.

RAGLAN—Neck Edge: With No. 13 needles, cast on 25 (27-27) sts. **Row 1:** P 1, k 1, * p 1, mark last st for seam st; k 1, p 1, k 1; p 1, mark last st for seam st; k 1, p 1 over next 11 (13-13) sts, ending k 1; p 1, mark last st for seam st; k 1, p 1, k 1; p 1, mark last st for seam st; k 1, p 1, cast on 2 (2-4) sts—27 (29-31) sts. **Row 2—right side:** K 3 (3-5), inc in each of next 2 sts, k 2, inc in each of next 2 sts, k 10 (12-12); inc in each of next 2 sts; k 2, inc in each of next 2 sts, k 2; cast on 2 (2-4) sts—37 (39-43) sts. **Row 3:** K 1, * p 1, k 1; repeat from * across, cast on 4 sts—41 (43-47) sts. **Row 4:** * K to within 1 st of seam st, inc in each of next 2 sts; repeat from * 3 times, k to end of row, cast on 4 sts—53 (55-59) sts. **Row 5:** P 1, * k 1, p 1; repeat from * across. **Row 6—Buttonhole Row:** * K to within 1 st of seam st, inc in each of next 2 sts; repeat from * 3 times, k to last 5 sts, bind off next 3 sts, k 1. **Row 7:** K 1, p 1, cast on 3 sts over the bound-off sts, * p 1, k 1; repeat from * across—61 (63-67) sts. **Row 8:** * K to within 1 st of seam st, inc in next 2 sts; repeat from * 3 times, k to end of row—69 (71-75) sts. **Row 9:** P 1, * k 1, p 1; repeat from * across. **Row 10:** Same as row 8. **Row 11:** K 1, * p 1, k 1; repeat from * across. Repeating buttonholes every 13-14 (15-16—17-18) rows, work rows 8, 9, 10 and 11 until there are 141 (159-179) sts. Work even for 4 (2-0) rows. **Dividing Row—wrong side:** Work 22 (24-28) sts, place sts on a holder for right front; work 29 (33-37) sts for sleeve, place sts on a holder; work 39 (45-49) sts for back; place sts on a holder; work next 29 (33-37) sts; slip remaining 22 (24-28) sts on a holder for left front.

LEFT SLEEVE: Continuing pat, cast on 2 sts at beg of next 2 rows—33 (37-41) sts. Work even for 6 rows. Dec 1 st each side and repeat decs every 8th row 3 (4-5) times—25 (27-29) sts. Work even until 10 (12-14)" from underarm or desired length. End on wrong side. Bind off as to knit.

RIGHT SLEEVE: With right side to you, work across sts of sleeve and complete to correspond to left sleeve. Sew sleeve seams.

BODY: Attach yarn at left underarm, work pat across 22 (24-28) sts of left front. Work across sts of left front, pick up 3 sts along sleeve seam; work across 39 (45-49) sts of back; pick up 3 sts along sleeve seam, work 22 (24-28) sts of right front—89 (99-111) sts. Repeating buttonholes until 4 have been made, continue in pat until 6 (7-8)" from underarms. End on wrong side.
Pocket Openings: Work 12 (14-16) sts; work next 12 (14-14) sts and slip them to a holder; work to last 24 (28-30) sts; work 12 (14-14) sts and slip them to a holder, complete row. On next row cast on 12 (14-14) sts over each pocket opening and continue in pat until piece measures 10½ (12½-14)" from underarms or desired length. End on wrong side. Bind off as to k.

POCKET LININGS: Slip sts of lining to No. 13 needles and continue in pat for 3 (3½-4)". End on wrong side. Bind off as to k.

COLLAR: Cast on 29 (31-33) sts. P 1 row. K next row inc 8 sts evenly spaced—37 (39-41) sts. Work even in pat for 4 (4½-4½)". End on wrong side. Bind off as to k.

FINISHING: Sew cast-on edge of collar to neck edge, leaving 4 (5-5) sts free at each front edge. Sew pocket linings to wrong side. Finish buttonholes with blanket st.

CROCHETED EDGE—Row 1: With right side to you, starting at side edge of collar on left front neck edge, work 4 (5-5) sc over the 4 (5-5) free sts at front, work 2 sc in corner, keeping edge even, and working 2 sc in each corner, continue sc down left front, along lower edge and up right front to collar. Fasten off. **Row 2:** Starting at left front edge as before, sl st in each sc of previous row. Fasten off. Work same 2 rows of edging on side and outer edges of collar and along lower edge of sleeves and top of pockets. Steam-press lightly.

Crocheted Cap with Mohair Trim

shown on page 149
Sizes Small, Medium, Large

Directions are for small size. Changes for medium and large sizes are in parentheses.
COLUMBIA-MINERVA "Calibar" and "Roma" were used for the original model.

MATERIALS: Bulky Quick Knit Yarn—2 (2-3) ozs. Mohair—1 oz for trim.
Crochet Hook: No. H.

GAUGE—The Most Important Word in Crochet
2½ dc = 1"; 1 row dc = ⅞".
Easy-to-follow crochet instructions are in the "How-To Section"—pages 196-199.

Starting at top ch 5. Join with sl st to form a ring. **Rnd 1:** Ch 3, make 9 dc in ring. Join with sl st in top of ch-3. **Rnd 2:** Ch 3, dc in joining, 2 dc in each dc around (20 dc, counting ch-3 as 1 dc). Join. **Rnd 3:** Ch 3, 2 dc in next dc, * dc in next dc, 2 dc in next dc; repeat from * around (30 dc). Join. **Rnd 4:** Ch 3, dc in next dc, 2 dc in next dc, * dc in each of next 2 dc, 2 dc in next dc; repeat from * around—on small size only omit last inc—39 (40-40) dc. **Rnd 5:** Ch 3, dc in each dc around inc 0 (2-5) dc evenly spaced—39 (42-45) dc. Join. Work around and around in dc until cap measures 6 (7-7)" or desired depth. Fasten off.

TRIM—Rnd 1: Attach Mohair just below the *edge* of last row. Sc around each dc just below edge. Join to first sc. **Rnd 2:** * Ch 5, skip 2 sc, sc in next sc; repeat from * until there are 12 (13-14) ch-5 loops, ch 2, dc in joining—13 (14-15) loops. **Rnds 3 and 4:** * Ch 5, sc in next loop; repeat from * around, ending ch 2, dc in dc of last loop. Fasten off.
* Cut a strand of Mohair 20" long. Double this strand. Insert hook under a ch-5 and draw center of double strand part way through, forming a loop, catch ends and draw them through this loop; carry ends to top of cap and fasten. Repeat from * around, spacing strands evenly and keeping them just loose enough to maintain depth of cap.

Crocheted Cap instructions are on page 148.

POMPON: Wrap remaining Mohair around a 4" cardboard about 40 times. Remove from cardboard, tie securely in center. Cut loops and trim. Sew to top of cap.

Pattern Stitch Pullover instructions are on page 151.
Bordered Pullover instructions are on page 153.

Pattern Stitch Pullover

shown at left on page 150
Sizes 4, 6, 8, 10, 12, 14

Directions are for size 4. Changes for sizes 6, 8, 10, 12 and 14 are in parentheses.
BERNAT "Nylo Sports" was used for the original model.

MATERIALS: Nylon and Wool Sports Yarn—or—Sayelle Nantuk of Sports Yarn weight: 10 (12-12-14-16-16) ozs.
Knitting Needles: 1 pr each of No. 3 and No. 5 or size required to knit to gauge.

GAUGE—The Most Important Word in Knitting
6 sts = 1"; 8 rows = 1".
Detailed drawings of how to make all of the basic stitches and all abbreviations used in these directions appear in the "How-To Section"—pages 169-210.

TEST PIECE: With No. 5 needles, cast on 18 sts. Work in pat for 24 rows. Piece should measure 3 × 3 inches. If too small, try larger-size needles; if too large, try smaller-size needles until correct gauge is obtained. While knitting, measure your work frequently to be sure you are maintaining the gauge.

MEASUREMENTS: Chest—24 (26-28-30-32-34)"; across back and front at underarms—12 (13-14-15-16-17)"; sleeve width at upper-arm—9½ (10-11-11½-12-12½)".

PATTERN STITCH—Multiple of 4 sts plus 2.
Row 1—right side: K 2, * p 2, k 2; repeat from * across. **Row 2:** Purl. **Row 3:** P 2, * k 2, p 2; repeat from * across. **Row 4:** Purl. Repeat these 4 rows for pat.

BACK: With No. 3 needles, cast on 72 (76-84-88-96-100) sts. K 2, p 2 in ribbing for 1½ (2-2-2-2-2½-2½)". On last row inc 1 st each end of row—74 (78-86-90-98-102) sts. K 1 row, p 1 row. Change to No. 5 needles. Work even in pat until piece measures 9 (10-11-11½-12-12)" or desired length to underarms.

Raglan Armholes: Bind off 2 (3-3-3-4-4) sts at beg of next 2 rows. **Dec Row**: K 2, sl 1, k 1, psso, work to last 4 sts, k 2 tog, k 2. Purl 1 row. Repeat last 2 rows until 26 (26-28-28-30-30) sts remain. Bind off loosely.

FRONT: Work same as back until piece measures 1" less than back to underarms. End with a p row.
Neck and Raglan Shaping: Work across 34 (36-40-42-46-48) sts, k 2 tog; slip next 2 sts to a safety pin and remaining sts to a holder. Working on sts of one side, dec 1 st at neck edge every 4th row 10 (10-11-11-12-12) times more—**meanwhile**—when the same length as back to underarm, from arm edge bind off 2 (3-3-3-4-4) sts once. Work raglan shaping same as right side of back.

Leave 2 center sts on pin, attach yarn, k 2 tog, complete row. Work to correspond to other side, making raglan decs same as left side of back.

SLEEVES: With No. 3 needles, cast on 40 (44-44-48-48-52) sts. K 2, p 2 in ribbing for 2 (2-2½-3-3-3)". On last row inc 6 sts evenly spaced—46 (50-50-54-54-58) sts. Change to No. 5 needles. Work in pat for 1". Keeping continuity of pat, inc 1 st each side every 6th row 5 (5-8-8-10-10) times—56 (60-66-70-74-78) sts. Work even until sleeve measures 10½ (11½-12-12½-13½-15)" or desired length to underarm.
Raglan shaping: Bind off 3 (4-4-4-4-4) sts at beg of next 2 rows. Work raglan shaping same as back until 6 sts remain. Bind off.

FINISHING: Steam-press pieces lightly. Sew left sleeve to back and front, sew right sleeve to front only.

NECKBAND: With right side to you using No. 3 needles, pick up 26 (26-28-28-30-30) sts across back of neck; 6 sts across top of sleeve; 36 (40-40-42-44-48) sts along left side of neck; slip a marker on needle, k 2 sts from pin, slip a marker on needle; pick up 36 (40-40-42-44-48) sts along other side of neck and 6 sts across top of sleeve—112 (120-122-126-132-140) sts. Knit 1 row on wrong side. **Row 2**: K, dec 1 st before first and after 2nd marker. **Row 3**: Purl. Repeat rows 2 and 3 once more. Work in k 2, p 2 ribbing, always knitting the 2 center sts on right side and dec 1 st before first and after 2nd marker every other row until there are 6 rows of ribbing. Bind off in ribbing, dec 2 sts as before.

Sew right sleeve to back and neckband edges tog. Sew underarm and sleeve seams.

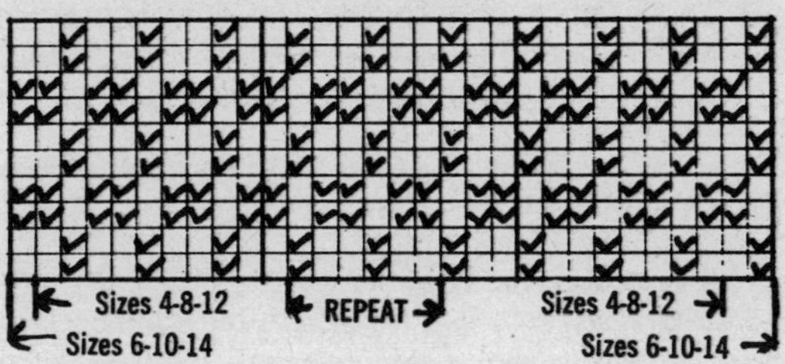

Bordered Pullover

shown at right on page 150
Sizes 4, 6, 8, 10, 12, 14

Directions are for size 4. Changes for sizes 6, 8, 10, 12 and 14 are in parentheses.
BERNAT "Nylo Sports" was used for the original model.

MATERIALS: Nylon and Wool of Sports Yarn—or—Sayelle Nantuk of Sports Yarn weight: 10 (12-12-14-16-16) ozs of Main Color (MC); 2 ozs of Contrasting Color (CC).
Knitting Needles: 1 pr each of No. 3 and No. 5 or size required to knit to gauge.

GAUGE—The Most Important Word in Knitting
6 sts = 1"; 8 rows = 1".
Detailed drawings of how to make all of the basic stitches and all abbreviations used in these directions appear in the "How-To Section"—pages 169-210.

TEST PIECE: With No. 5 needles, cast on 18 sts. Work in stockinette st (k 1 row, p 1 row) for 24 rows. Piece should measure 3 × 3 inches. If too small, try larger-size needles; if too large, try smaller-size needles until correct gauge is obtained. While knitting, measure your work frequently to be sure you are maintaining the gauge.

MEASUREMENTS: Chest—24 (26-28-30-32-34)"; across back and front at underarms—12 (13-14-15-16-17)"; sleeve width at upper-arm—9½ (10-11-11½-12-12½)".

Note: When changing colors while working design, always bring the color to be used from under and around the color just dropped. This will twist yarns and prevent a hole in work.

BACK: With No. 3 needles and MC, cast on 72 (76-84-88-96-100) sts. K 1, p 1 in ribbing for 1½ (1½-2-2-2-2½)". On last row inc 1 st each end of needle—74 (78-86-90-98-102) sts. Change to No. 5 needles. K 1 row, p 1 row. Work even in stockinette st following chart until completed. Continue with MC until piece measures 9 (10½-11½-12-12½-12½)" or desired length to underarms.
Raglan Armholes: Bind off 2 (3-3-3-4-4) sts at beg of next 2 rows. **Dec. Row** K 2, sl 1, k 1, psso, k to last 4 sts, k 2 tog, k 2. Purl 1 row. Repeat last 2 rows until 26 (26-28-28-30-30) sts remain. Bind off loosely.

FRONT: Work same as back until piece measures 1" less than back to underarms.
Neck and Raglan Shaping: Work across 34 (36-40-42-46-48) sts, k 2 tog; slip next 2 sts to a safety pin and remaining sts to a holder. Working on sts of one side, dec 1 st at neck edge every 4th row 10 (10-11-11-12-12) times—**meanwhile**—when same length as back to underarm, from side edge bind off 2 (3-3-3-4-4) sts once. Work raglan shaping same as right side of back.

Leave center 2 sts on pin, attach yarn, k 2 tog, complete row. Work to correspond to other side, making raglan decs same as for left side of back.

SLEEVES: With No. 3 needles, cast on 40 (44-44-48-48-52) sts. K 1, p 1 in ribbing for 2 (2-2½-2½-3-3)". On last row inc 4 (4-6-6-8-8) sts evenly spaced—44 (48-50-54-56-60) sts. Change to No. 5 needles. K 1 row, p 1 row. Work even following chart until completed. Inc 1 st each side and repeat incs every 6th row 6 (6-8-8-9-9) times—56 (60-66-70-74-78) sts. Work even until sleeve measures 10½ (11½-12½-13½-15½)" or desired length.
Raglan Shaping: Bind off 3 (4-4-4-4-4) sts at beg of next 2 rows. Work raglan shaping same as back until 6 sts remain. Bind off.

FINISHING: Steam-press pieces lightly. Sew left sleeve to front and back, sew right sleeve to front only.

NECKBAND: *Instructions are on page 77.*

Spiral Mittens

shown on page 156
Sizes Small, Medium, Large

Directions are for small size. Changes for medium and large sizes are in parentheses.
COATS & CLARK'S "Red Heart Knitting Worsted" was used for the original model.

MATERIALS: Knitting Worsted–2 (3-3) ozs.
Knitting Needles: 1 pr each of No. 4 and No. 7 or size required to knit to gauge.

GAUGE–The Most Important Word in Knitting
6 sts = 1″; 6 rows = 1″.

MEASUREMENTS: Around palm–5 (6-7)″; length from cuff to fingertips–5 (6-6¾)″.

PATTERN STITCH–Multiple of 3 sts.
Row 1—right side: Skip first 2 sts, pass right-hand needle in back of these 2 sts and k in back loop of 3rd st, leave st on left-hand needle, k in the front loop of first and 2nd sts, drop 3rd st (first knitted st) from left-hand needle (cross st made), * work cross st over next 3 sts; repeat from * across. **Row 2 and all even rows:** Purl. **Row 3:** K 1, * cross st over next 3 sts; repeat from *, ending k 2. **Row 5:** K 2; * cross st over next 3 sts; repeat from *, ending k 1. **Row 6:** Purl. Repeat these 6 rows for pat.

RIGHT MITTEN—Cuff: With No. 7 needles, cast on 30 (36-42) sts. With No. 4 needles, k 1, p 1 in ribbing for 2½ (3-3)″. Change to No. 7 needles. P 1 row inc 3 sts evenly spaced–33 (39-45) sts. **Thumb Gore—Row 1:** Work row 1 of pat across 15 (18-21) sts; place a marker on needle, p and k in next st (inc), k in front and back loop of next st (inc), p 1, place a marker on needle; work pat over remaining 15 (18-21) sts. **Row 2 and all even rows:** P to marker and slip, k 1, p to 1 st before next marker, k 1, slip marker, p to end of row. Always slip markers each row. **Row 3:** K 1, cross
(Continued on p. 156)

st to within 2 sts of marker, k 2; p and k in next st, k 2, k in front and back loop of next st, p 1; k 1, continue pat across, ending k 2. **Row 4**: As row 2. Continue as rows 3 and 4, inc 1 st after first marker and in 2nd st before 2nd marker until there are 9 (11-13) sts between markers. End with a p row.

Thumb: Work pat to first marker; k to 2nd marker; remove marker. Turn. **Row 2**: Inc in first st, p to within 1 st of marker, inc in next st, remove marker—11 (13-15) sts. Work in stockinette st (k 1 row, p 1 row) over these sts for 1¾ (2-2¼)" or until ¼" less than desired thumb length. End with a p row. * K 1, k 2 tog; repeat from * across row. Break yarn, leaving 10" end. Draw yarn through sts, pull up tight and fasten. Sew seam on wrong side.

Hand: With right side to you, attach yarn in last st worked on right-hand needle, cast on 3 sts, work in pat across palm of hand—33 (39-45) sts. Continue in pat until 5 (6-6¾)" above ribbing or ½" less than desired finished length. End with a p row.

Shaping—Row 1: Working in pat, at each cross st, * skip 2 sts, k in back loop of next st, k the 2 skipped sts tog (1 st dec); repeat from * across. P 1 row. **Row 3**: * K in back loops of next 2 sts (dec); repeat from * across. Break yarn leaving 20" end. Draw end through sts and pull up tight, fasten securely. Sew side seam matching rows. Sew base of thumb along cast on sts.

Make left mitten the same. Steam-press lightly.

Jacket and Beret

shown on page 158
Sizes 4, 6, 8

Directions are for size 4. Changes for sizes 6 and 8 are in parentheses.
COATS & CLARK'S "Red Heart Knitting Worsted" was used for the original model.

MATERIALS: Knitting Worsted or Orlon Yarn of Knitting Worsted weight. Main Color (MC) 9 (10-12) ozs; Contrasting Color (CC) –9 (10-12) ozs. 4 buttons.
Knitting Needles: 1 pr each of No. 5 and No. 9 or size required to knit to gauge.

GAUGE–The Most Important Word in Knitting
9 sts = 2"; 9 rows = 1".
Detailed drawings of how to make all of the basic stitches and all abbreviations used in these directions appear in the "How-To Section"–pages 169-210.

TEST PIECE: With No. 7 needles and MC, cast on 19 sts. Work in pat for 27 rows. Piece should measure 4 × 3 inches. If too small, try larger-size needles; if too large, try smaller-size needles until correct gauge is obtained. While knitting, measure your work frequently to be sure you are maintaining the gauge.
(Continued on p. 159)

Jacket and Beret instructions are on page 157.

MEASUREMENTS: At chest, buttoned—27 (29-31)"; across back at underarms—13 (14-15)"; across each front at underarms—8 (9-10)"; sleeve width at upperarm—10 (11-11½)".

PATTERN STITCH—Multiple of 2 sts plus 1.
Row 1—right side: With CC, k 1, * with yarn in back, sl 1, k 1; repeat from * across. **Row 2**: With CC, p 1, * with yarn in front sl 1, p 1; repeat from * across. **Rows 3 and 4**: With MC, knit. **Rows 5 and 6**: With CC, knit. **Rows 7 and 8**: With MC, knit. Repeat these 8 rows for pat, taking care to keep slip sts over same sts when shaping.

NOTE: Jacket is worked lengthwise.

RIGHT FRONT: Starting at front edge with No. 9 needles and MC, cast on 55 (59-65) sts. With MC, k 1 row. Attach CC and work even in pat until piece measures 4¼ (4¾-5½)". End on wrong side at upper edge.
Armhole: Keeping continuity of pat, dec 1 st at upper edge every other row 15 (17-19) times. Work even for 2 (2-4) rows. End at upper edge.

BACK: Inc 1 st at beg of next row and repeat inc every other row 14 (16-18) times—55 (59-65) sts. Work even until 6½ (6¾-7¼)" from last inc row. Work 2nd armhole same as first.

LEFT FRONT: Work even until 1 pat row less than right front. End with row 3 of pat. With MC, bind off knitting all sts.

SLEEVES: Starting at underarms with No. 9 needles and MC, cast on 35 (41-49) sts. **Short Rows—Rows 1 and 2**: With MC, k 6, turn; k 6. **Rows 3 and 4**; With CC, k 12, turn; k 12. **Rows 5 and 6**: With MC, inc in first st, k 17, turn; k 19. **Row 7**: With CC, inc in first st, * sl 1, k 1; repeat from * 11 times more—26 sts on right hand needle, turn. **Row 8**: Work pat across. **Row 9**: Inc in first st, k across all sts. **Row 10**: Knit. Continue in pat, inc 1 st at upper edge every other row until there are 49 (57-65) sts. Work even until 2½" from last inc row. Continue pat, dec 1 st at upper edge every other row 12 (14-14) times. Continuing to dec 1 st at upper edge every other row twice more, at lower edge bind off 6 sts every other row 4 times. Bind off remaining sts.

(Continued on p. 160)

CUFF: With right side to you, using No. 5 needles and CC, pick up 36 (40-44) sts along lower edge of sleeve. K 2, p 2 in ribbing for 1 (1½-1¾)". Bind off in ribbing.
Steam-press pieces lightly. Seam sleeves. Sew shaped edges of sleeves to correspond to armhole edges of body.

YOKE: With right side to you, using No. 9 needles and MC, pick up 89 (99-109) sts along entire upper edge of jacket. **Row 1**: Knit. **Row 2**: With CC, k 2, bind off next 2 sts, k 4, bind off next 2 sts (double buttonholes), k remaining sts. **Row 3**: With CC, k, casting on 2 sts over each set of bound-off sts. Work 4 rows of pattern. Continue in pat, dec 6 sts evenly spaced on next row and repeat decs every 4th row 3 (4-5) times more—65 (69-73) sts. Make another set of buttonholes on next 2 rows.
Neck and Collar: Bind off 6 sts at beg of next row; 5 sts at beg of next row—54 (58-62) sts. Change to No. 5 needles. **Row 1**: With CC, k 2, * p 2, k 2; repeat from * across. **Row 2**: P 2, * k 2, p 2; repeat from * across. Repeat these 2 rows for 1". Change to No. 9 needles and continue until collar measures 2¾ (3-3¼)". Bind off loosely in ribbing.

FRONT BORDERS: With right side to you, using No. 9 needles and CC, starting at right lower edge, pick up 67 (73-79) sts to neck. With CC, k 2 rows. With MC, k 1 row. Bind off with MC. Work left front the same, starting at neck edge.

LOWER BORDER: With right side to you, using No. 9 needles and CC, pick up about 140 (150-160) sts all along lower edge of jacket. Increasing 1 st each side every row, work border as for fronts. Sew ends of rows to corresponding rows of front borders. Work buttonhole st around buttonholes. Steam-press lightly. Sew on buttons.

BERET

With No. 5 needles and CC, cast on 80 (84-88) sts. K 2, p 2 in ribbing for 1 (1¼-1¼)". Inc 1 st at end of last row. Change to No. 9 needles. Starting with row 4 of pat, inc 6 sts evenly spaced every 4th row 2 (2-3) times. Work even in pat until piece measures 3 (3½-4)". Dec 6 st evenly spaced every 8th row twice; dec 10 sts every other row until 11 (15-15) sts remain. Do not dec on rows 1 and 2 of pat. Break yarn leaving 16" end. Draw through sts, pull up tight and fasten. Sew back seam. Trim with a pompon as pictured. Steam-press lightly.

Chevron Design Pullover for Him or Her

shown on page 162
Sizes 4, 6, 8, 10, 12, 14

Directions are for size 4. Changes for sizes 6, 8, 10, 12, and 14 are in parentheses.
BERNAT "Super Knitting Worsted" was used for the original model.

MATERIALS: Knitting Worsted—or—Nylon and Wool of Knitting Worsted weight. Main Color (MC)—10 (10-12-12-14-14) ozs; Contrasting Colors—A, B, and C—2 ozs of each color.
Knitting Needles: 1 pr each of No. 5 and No. 8 or size required to knit to gauge. 1 set of No. 5 dp needles for Boy's turtleneck.

GAUGE—The Most Important Word in Knitting
5 sts = 1"; 7 rows = 1".
Detailed drawings of how to make all of the basic stitches and all abbreviations used in these directions appear in the "How-To Section"—pages 169-210.

TEST PIECE: With No. 8 needles and MC, cast on 15 sts. Work in stockinete st (k 1 row, p 1 row) for 21 rows. Piece should measure 3 × 3 inches. If too small, try larger-size needles; if too large, try smaller-size needles until correct gauge is obtained. While knitting, measure your work frequently to be sure you are maintaining the gauge.

MEASUREMENTS: At chest—24 (26-27½-29½-31½-34½)"; across back at underarms—12 (13-13-14½-15½-17)"; across front at underarms—12 (13-14½-15-16-17½)"; sleeve width at upperarm—10 (11-11-12-12-13½)".

NOTE: While working design, always bring the color to be used from under and around the color just dropped; this will twist yarns and avoid a hole in work.
(Continued on p. 163)

Chevron Design Pullover for Him or Her instructions are on page 161.

BACK: With No. 5 needles and MC, cast on 60 (64-64-72-76-80) sts. K 2, p 2 in ribbing for 1½ (1½-2-2-2½-2½)". On last row inc 1 (3-3-1-3-5) sts evenly spaced—61 (67-67-73-79-85) sts. Change to No. 8 needles. Work in stockinette st (k 1 row, p 1 row) until piece measures 4 (4½-6-6-7-7)". Attach A. Work even following chart until 10 rows of B have been completed.

Raglan Armholes: Keeping continuity of design, bind off 2 sts at beg of next 2 rows. Dec 1 st each side every 4th row 2 (2-4-3-4-4) times; every other row until 25 (27-27-27-29-29) sts remain. Bind off.

FRONT: With No. 5 needles and MC, cast on 60 (64-72-76-80-88) sts. Work ribbing same as back. On last row inc 1 (3-1-3-5-3) sts evenly spaced—61 (67-73-79-85-91) sts. Work same as back to underarms, ending on same pat row.

Raglan Armholes: Bind off 2 sts at beg of next 2 rows. Dec 1 st every 4th row 2 (2-2-1-2-2) times; every other row until 35 (39-39-41-41-41) sts remain. End with a k row.

Neck: On next p row bind off center 13 (15-17-17-19-19) sts. Working on sts of one side, at neck edge dec 1 st every other row 4 times, continuing raglan decs until 2 sts remain. K 2 tog. Attach yarn at opposite neck edge and work other side to correspond.

(Continued on p. 164)

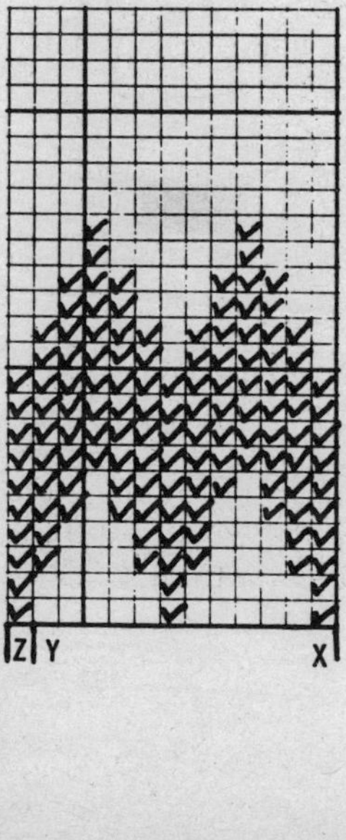

Starting at X, work to Y, repeat between X and Y across, ending at Z. Read chart from right to left on k rows and from left to right on p rows. * Work 16 rows of chart with A, then work 6 (6-8-8-8-8) rows with MC. Repeat from *, using Colors B and C on 2nd and 3rd stripes. Complete pullover with MC.

Chevron Design Pullover with a turtleneck is also ideal for a boy.

SLEEVES: With No. 5 needles and MC, cast on 36 (40-40-44-48-48) sts. K 2, p 2 in ribbing for 1½ (1½-2-2-2½-2½)". On last row inc 1 (3-5-3-1-5) sts evenly spaced. Change to No. 8 needles. Work in stockinette st, inc 1 st each side every ½" 6 (6-5-7-6-7) times—49 (55-55-61-61-67) sts. Work even until sleeve measures 6 (6-7-8-9-10)". Work even following chart until 10 rows of B have been completed. End on same pat row as back.

Raglan Shaping: Bind off 2 sts at beg of next 2 rows. Dec 1 st each side every 4th row 1 (0-2-1-4-4) times; every other row until 13 sts remain. Dec 1 st each side every row twice. Bind off remaining 9 sts.

FINISHING: Steam-press pieces lightly. Sew sleeves to front and back. Sew underarm and sleeve seams.

GIRL'S COLLAR: With No. 5 needles and MC, cast on 84 (84-88-92-92-96) sts. **Row 1**: K 1, (p 1, k 1) 3 times; p 2, * k 2, p 2; repeat from * to last 7 sts, k 1, (p 1, k 1) 3 times. **Row 2**: P 1, (k 1, p 1) 3 times; k 2, * p 2, k 2; repeat from * to last 7 sts, p 1, (k 1, p 1) 3 times. Repeat these 2 rows once. **Buttonhole Row**: Work 4 sts, bind off next 2 sts, complete row. On next row cast on 2 sts over the bound-off sts. Continue ribbing as established until collar measures 4½ (4½-5-5-5½-5½)". Bind off in ribbing. Sew cast-on edge of collar to neck edge, taking care to have buttonhole on right side and lapping collar 1" at center front.

BOY'S TURTLENECK: With right side to you, using No. 5 dp needles and MC, pick up 76 (76-84-84-88-88) sts all around neck edge. K 2, p 2 around and around in ribbing for 4½ (4½-5-5-5½-5½)". Bind off loosely in ribbing.

Windbreaker

shown on this page
Sizes 8, 10, 12, 14

Directions are for size 8. Changes for sizes 10, 12 and 14 are in parentheses.
COLUMBIA-MINERVA "Nantuk Knitting Worsted" was used for the original model.

MATERIALS: Nantuk Knitting Worsted—or—Knitting Worsted: 16 (20-20-24) ozs. Jacket zipper for closing.
Knitting Needles: 1 pr each of No. 2 and No. 4. 29" Circular or
(Continued on p. 166)

Jumper needles or size required to knit to gauge. No. 00 steel crochet hook.

GAUGE—The Most Important Word in Knitting
6 sts = 1"; 8 rows = 1".
Detailed drawings of how to make all of the basic stitches and all abbreviations used in these directions appear in the "How-To Section"—pages 169-210.

TEST PIECE: With No. 4 straight needles, cast on 18 sts. Work in stockinette st (k 1 row, p 1 row) for 24 rows. Piece should measure 3 × 3 inches. If too small, try larger-size needles; if too large, try smaller-size needles until correct gauge is obtained. While knitting, measure your work frequently to be sure you are maintaining the gauge.

MEASUREMENTS: At chest, closed—30 (32-34-36)"; sleeve width at upperarm—11 (11¾-12¼-13-13¾)".

RAGLAN SHAPING: Starting at neck edge with circular or jumper needle, cast on 80 (84-88-92) sts. Work back and forth in stockinette st. **Row 1—wrong side:** K 4, p 11 (12-13-14), slip a marker on needle (right front); p 10, slip a marker on needle (right sleeve); p 30 (32-34-36), slip a marker on needle (back); p 10, slip a marker on needle (left sleeve); p 11 (12-13-14), k 4 (left front). **Row 2:** * K to 1 st before marker, inc in next st, slip marker, inc in next st; repeat from * 3 times more, k to end of row. **Row 3:** K 4, p across slipping markers to last 4 sts, k 4. Repeat rows 2 and 3, increasing 8 sts every k row 29 (31-33-35) times more—320 (340-360-380) sts. There are 45 (48-51-54) sts on each front; 70 (74-78-82) sts on each sleeve and 90 (96-102-108) sts across back. End with a p row at left front. **Dividing Row:** K across 45 (48-51-54) sts of left front, slip these sts to a holder; with No. 4 straight needle, k across 70 (74-78-82) sts of sleeve. Leave remaining sts on needle.

LEFT SLEEVE: Continue in stockinette st for 2". Dec 1 st each side and repeat decs every ¾" 8 times more—52 (56-60-64) sts. Work even until sleeve measures 11 (12-14-16)" or 4" less than finished length, allowing for turn-back of cuff. On last row dec 4 (6-6-8) sts evenly spaced—48 (50-54-56) sts. Change to No. 2 needles. K 1, p 1 in ribbing for 4". Bind off loosely in ribbing. Seam sleeve.

RIGHT SLEEVE: With right side to you, k across sts of sleeve and complete to correspond to left sleeve.

BODY: Attach yarn at left underarm of back, k across 90 (96-102-108) sts and across 45 (48-51-54) sts of right front. **Next Row:** K 4, p across to left underarm of back; p across 41 (44-47-50) sts of left front, k 4—180 (192-204-216) sts. Keeping 4 sts at each front edge in garter st, work even for 3 (3½-4-4½)". End with a p row. **Pocket Opening:** K 13 (14-15-16) sts; slip next 27 sts to a thread; cast on 27 sts; k to last 40 (41-42-43) sts; slip next 27 sts to a thread; cast on 27 sts; k last 13 (14-15-16) sts—180 (192-204-216) sts. Work even until 7½ (8½-9½-10)" from underarm or 4" less than desired finished length. End with a p row, decreasing 1 st in center of row. Change to No. 2 needles.
Ribbing—Row 1—right side: K 4, p 1, * k 1, p 1; repeat from * to last 4 sts, k 4. **Row 2:** K 5, * p 1, k 1; repeat from * to last 6 sts, p 1, k 5. Repeat these 2 rows for 4". Bind off loosely.

POCKET LININGS: Slip sts from thread to needle and continue in stockinette st for 3½ (4-4½-5)". Bind off.

POCKET TABS: With right side to you using No. 2 needles, pick up 29 sts about ¼" *above* pocket opening. **Row 1:** K 1, * p 1, k 1; repeat from * across. **Row 2:** P 1, * k 1, p. 1; repeat from * across. Repeat these 2 rows for 1". **Buttonhole:** Rib 13, bind off 3 sts, rib to end of row. On next row cast on 3 sts over the bound-off sts. Keeping continuity of ribbing, bind off 2 sts at beg of **every** row until 1 st remains. Work 1 row sc around tab and across pocket opening.

COLLAR: With right side to you, using No. 2 needles, pick up 31 (31-35-35) sts across back of neck. Work in k 1, p 1 ribbing (as on pocket tab), picking up 2 sts on neck edge at end of **every** row until there are 81 (85-89-93) sts and row begins and ends at front edges. P 1 row on right side for turning ridge. Bind off 2 sts at beg of **every** row until 31 (31-35-35) sts remain. Bind off in ribbing.

FINISHING: Fold collar in half on turning ridge to wrong side and sew bound-off edge to neck edge along picked-up row. Sew pocket linings to wrong side. Steam-press lightly. Sew zipper in place.

How-To Section

Even if you have knitted for years, you may find helpful suggestions in the following pages. If you are a beginner you will be amazed at how quickly you can become an expert.

All you really have to know is how to cast on (set up the required number of stitches on the needle), knit, purl and bind off (finish off the stitches so that they won't rip). By combining these basic stitches you will be able to do all simple knitting. Cables look complicated, but they are really very easy. Lace patterns are slightly more difficult, but they are just knitting and purling, with a few increases and decreases thrown in.

If you are a beginner, start with heavy yarn and No. 8 needles, so that you can see the stitches clearly. Cast on about twenty stitches and work in stockinette stitch until you have acquired enough confidence to handle the yarn and needles with ease. Then try out the other stitches in this chapter. If you drop a stitch don't get nervous, you'll find a drawing of how to pick it up.

Once you have mastered the art of knitting there will be hours of pleasure in store for you. As a creative hobby, it is inexpensive, takes up little space and is as portable as a pocket radio.

KNITTING ACCESSORIES

Courtesy of *Susan Bates*

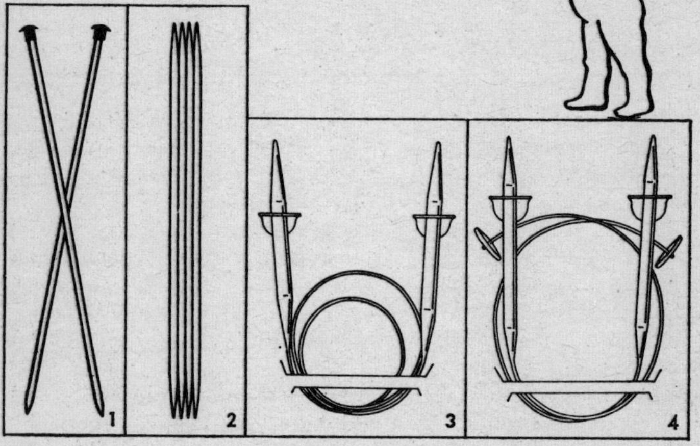

1–Single Point Knitting Needles are made of aluminum or plastic in sizes ranging from 0 through 15. The most popular lengths are 10 and 14 inches.

2–Double Point Needles are in sets of 4 in both aluminum or plastic. 7 inch lengths are available up to size 8. 10 inch lengths are available in sizes 0 through 8 in aluminum. Sizes 9, 10, 10½, 11, 13, and 15 come in plastic only.

3–Circular Needles are made 11-16-24-29-36 inches long. Sizes 0 through 5 have aluminum tips. All other sizes are made of nylon.

4–Jumper Needles of all DuPont nylon are excellent when working back and forth over a large number of stitches and when using bulky yarns. The weight of the work lays in the lap.

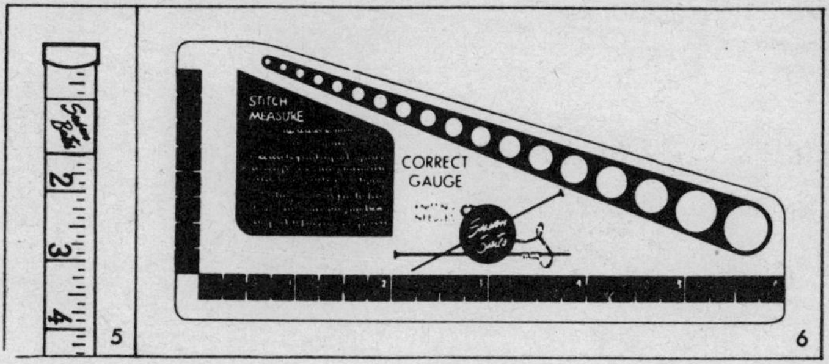

5–Tape Measure a must for all knitters.
6–Knit Check will check your gauge both for stitches and rows. It also checks the size of needles and has a 6-inch ruler.

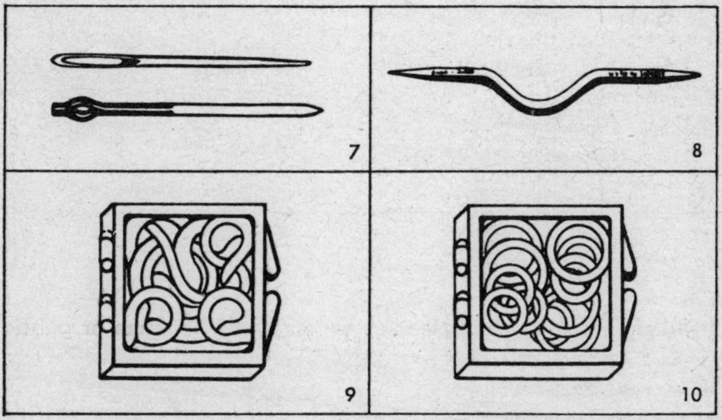

7–Yarn Needles in steel or plastic are necessary for sewing.
8–Cable Stitch Holder will prevent stitches from slipping while knitting cable stitch patterns.
9–Stitch Count Markers "Wafer Thin"–these plastic rings slip on any size needle where markers are needed.
10–Split Lock Stitch Count Markers are ideal for marking ends of rows and will fit all size needles wherever needed.

11

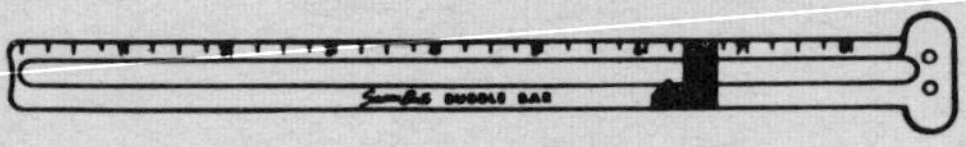

12

11—Stitch Holders are available from midget size, 1¾ inches to 10-inch lengths.

12—Bubble Bar will count stitches, magnify fine print a line at a time, act as a place marker and has a convenient 8-inch ruler. The sliding bar adjusts for spacing buttonholes.

13—Super Size Yarn Bobs are especially made for Bulky Yarns.

14—Yarn Bobs are used for argyle and multicolored knitting.

15—Point Protectors prevent stitches from slipping off needles when work is laid aside.

16—Pompon Maker has five interlocking rings for making various size pompons.

17—Knit Counts help you keep track of rows and are an excellent marker when work is laid aside.

13

14

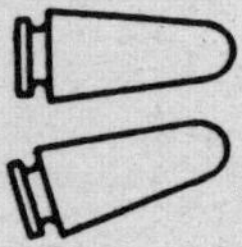

15

16

17

Gauge

THE MOST IMPORTANT WORD IN KNITTING

The tension at which the working strand of yarn is held, and the size of the needles, control and determine the size of your knitting. If you knit tightly (so the stitches are tight on your needle), you probably need larger needles. If you knit loosely (and the stitches slide too easily on the needle), you may need smaller needles. All directions are figured and written to a specified gauge. The knitter **must** maintain this gauge so that the finished piece will be the same as the measurements given. Often a knitter will get the stitch gauge and be off on the row gauge. In certain patterns this can affect the length required to complete increases and decreases. If you have this problem try using one size smaller needles on the purled side of your work. Row gauge is as important as stitch gauge for perfect knitting. Each set of directions gives a Test Piece. This will give you a chance to try out different needle sizes until your gauge is perfect. If you don't make the Test Piece (all professionals do) ycur gauge may be wrong and the finished garment will be too large or too small. Measure the overall width of your work frequently to be sure you are maintaining the correct gauge.

CASTING ON STITCHES—Fig. 1.

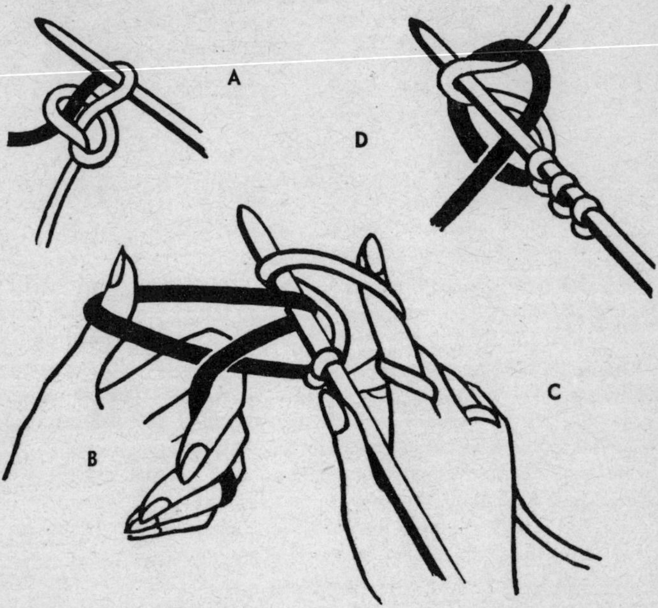

1ST METHOD—Fig. 1. Make a slip loop in yarn about 30 inches from end. Slip this loop on a needle and tighten. This is your first stitch (a). * With short end (shaded strand) make a loop on left thumb and insert needle from front to back (b), bring ball strand of yarn under and around needle (c), draw yarn through loop to form another stitch and tighten short end (d). Repeat from * for each stitch. Always cast on loosely. The length of the short end required for casting on varies according to the number of stitches, weight of yarn and size of needles. One yard of Baby Wool is sufficient for about 100 stitches when using No. 3 needles; however one yard of Knitting Worsted will only be enough for about 50 stitches on No. 8 needles. It is better to allow too much than to run short before you have finished casting on.

Fig. 2.

2ND METHOD—Fig. 2. Use this method when casting on at beginning of rows, for underlaps and for buttonholes or other cast-on stitches while work is in progress.

Reverse work if necessary so that the working strand hangs from the first stitch on left hand needle. * Insert point of right hand needle in the first stitch on left hand needle, pass yarn around point and draw the loop through (a), twist this loop to the left so that it lies in the same direction as the preceding stitches and slip it on the left hand needle to form a new stitch (b). Repeat from * as many times as specified, working into the loop of each new stitch on left hand needle. When all stitches have been cast on, reverse work and complete the row or round.

KNITTING—Fig. 3.

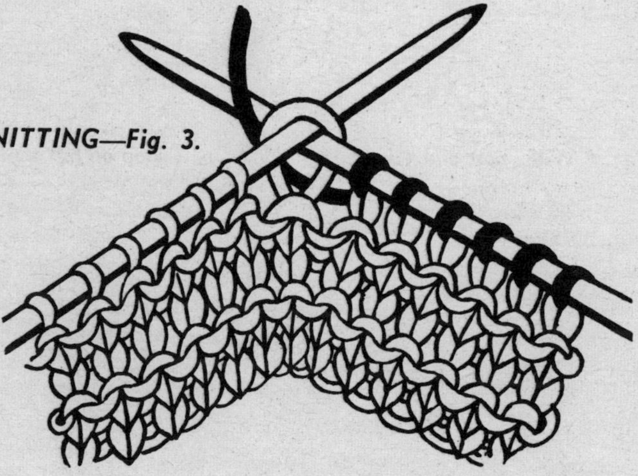

Hold needle with stitches in left hand, hold free needle between thumb and index finger of right hand or in the way you find most comfortable. Bring strand of yarn from ball over index finger, under middle finger and around little finger, or in any way that it can be controlled easily. * Insert needle from front to back in first stitch on left hand needle, pass yarn forward under needle and around to back, bring loop through the stitch toward you to form a new stitch on right hand needle, slip the stitch just worked off left hand needle. Repeat from * until all stitches are worked.

PURLING—Fig. 4.

* Holding yarn at front of right hand needle, insert point through stitch on left hand needle from **back to front,** pass yarn around point of needle from top to bottom, slip needle and loop through stitch to back, thus forming a new stitch on right hand needle, slip stitch just worked off left hand needle. Repeat from * until all stitches are worked.

GARTER STITCH—Fig. 5.

Knit every row.
2 rows make 1 ridge on each side of work.

STOCKINETTE ST—Fig. 6.

Knit side of work is right side.

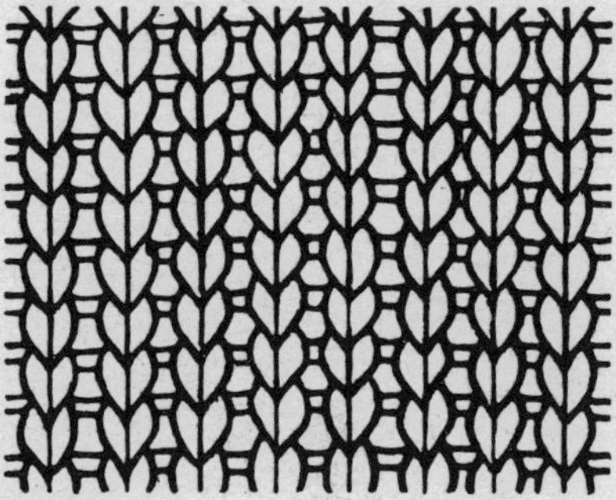

REVERSE STOCKINETTE ST—Fig. 7.

Purl side of work is used as right side.

STOCKINETTE STITCH—Fig. 8.

A

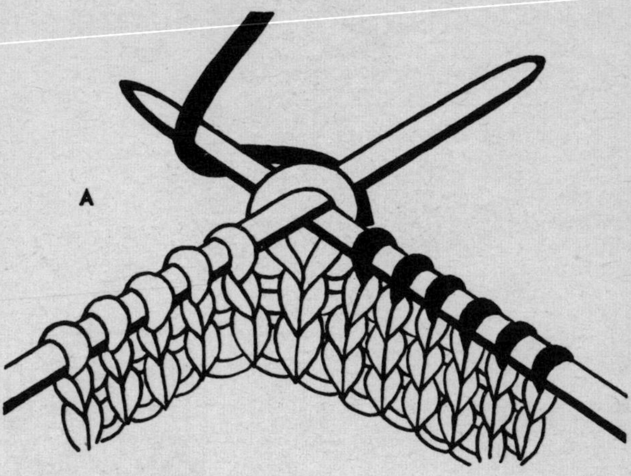

B

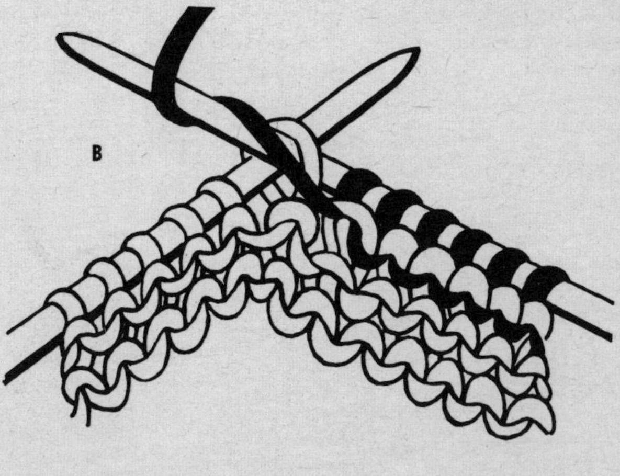

Knit 1 row (a). Purl 1 row (b).
Repeat these 2 rows.

RIBBING—Fig. 9.

A combination of knit and purl stitches forming vertical stripes. Always knit the knit and purl the purl stitches as they face you each row. When changing from knit to purl stitches bring the working strand of yarn under point of right hand needle to front of work; when changing from purl to knit stitches pass working strand of yarn under needle to back of work.

BINDING OFF—Fig. 10.

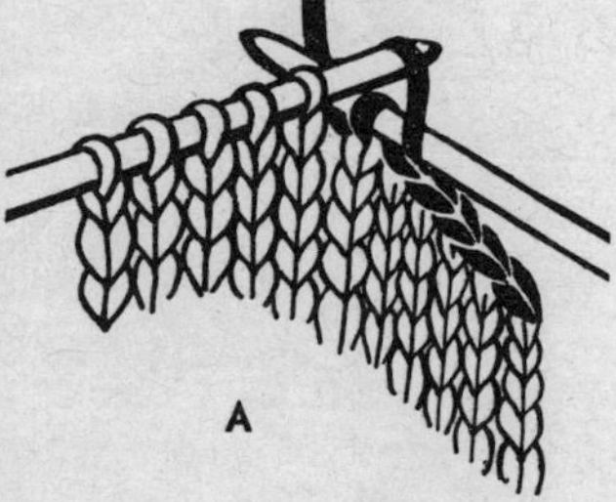

A

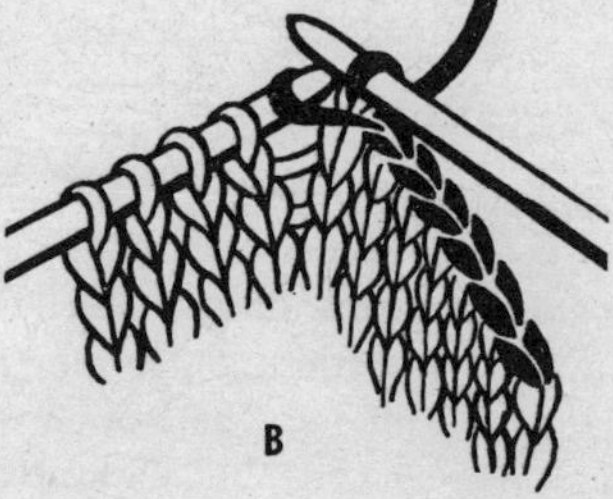

B

Knit or purl 2 stitches, * insert the point of left hand needle under the first stitch on right hand needle (a), lift this stitch over last stitch and off tip of needle (b). One stitch has been bound off. To bind off another stitch, knit another stitch and repeat from * as many times as specified. One stitch remains on right hand needle after binding off at the end of a row; break yarn and draw end through this stitch to fasten off. When binding off for buttonholes or pockets, the stitch is to be counted with the remaining stitches.

INCREASES—Fig. 11.

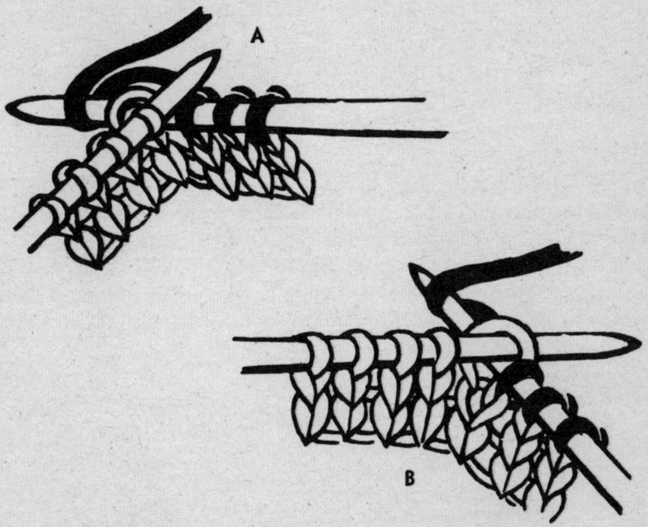

1ST METHOD—Fig. 11. Increases are made on the right side of work unless otherwise specified. Insert point of needle into the nub or loop in the back of the next stitch (a)—this is actually the top of the stitch of the preceding row—pass yarn around needle and draw loop through, forming a new stitch on right hand needle (b), now knit into the front loop of stitch on left hand needle in usual manner (b), then slip the stitch from left hand needle. When increasing on the purl side of work, insert needle from top of nub down into stitch of preceding row, purl the stitch, then purl the stitch on left hand needle.

INCREASES—Fig. 12.

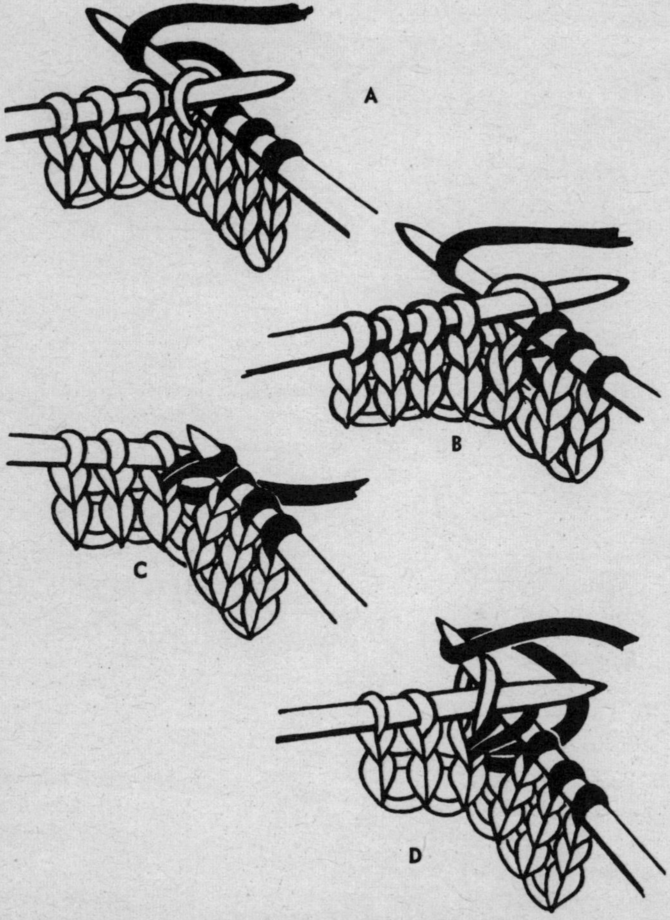

2ND METHOD—Fig. 12. Knit into the back loop of the next stitch (a), then knit into the front loop of the same stitch (b) and drop stitch from left hand needle. Sometimes instructions say to knit into the front (c) then into the back (d) of the same stitch. Use this method when increasing at beginning and end of rows.

DECREASES—Fig. 13.

B

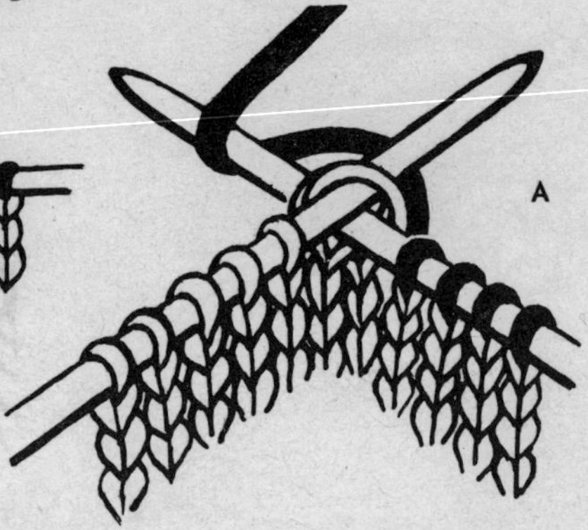

A

1ST METHOD—Fig. 13. Insert needle through 2 stitches on left hand needle and knit or purl as one stitch (a). This decrease will appear to slant to the right (b).

DECREASES—Fig. 14.

C

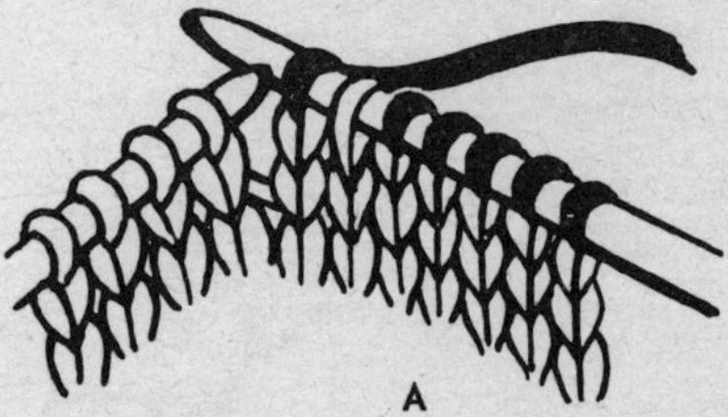

A

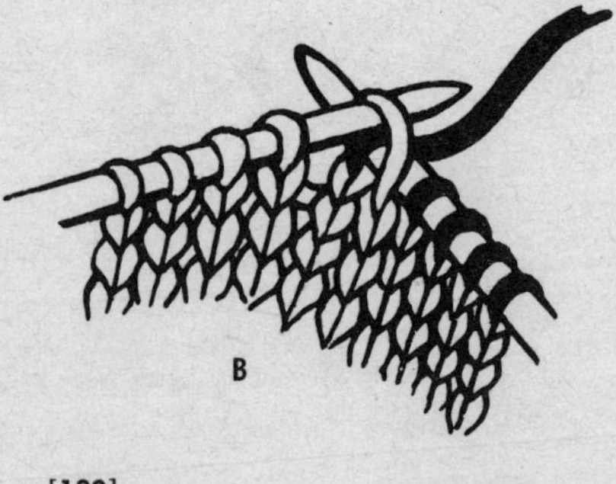

B

2ND METHOD—Fig. 14. Slip 1 stitch from left to right hand needle, knit the next stitch (a), then with point of left hand needle **pass the slipped stitch over** (abbreviated as psso) the last knit stitch and off point of right hand needle (b). This decrease will appear to slant to the left (c). The same slant to the left can be made by knitting into the **back** loops of 2 stitches (d).

YARN OVER—Fig. 15.

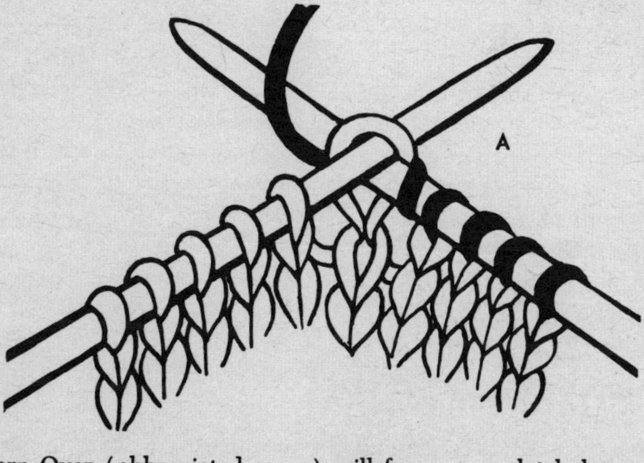

Yarn Over (abbreviated as yo) will form an eyelet hole or a hole in work for lace patterns or beading rows.

Yarn Over between knit stitches—Fig. 15. Bring yarn forward under point of right hand needle then up and over the top of the needle, knit the next stitch.

YARN OVER—Fig. 16.

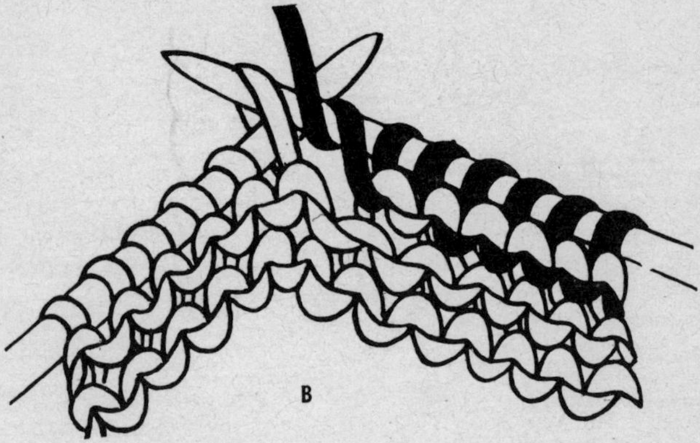

Yarn Over between purl stitches—Fig. 16. The yarn must be wrapped once completely around the right hand needle.
Yarn Over after a knit and before a purl stitch—bring the yarn forward and wrap completely around the right hand needle to bring the yarn to front of work again, then purl the stitch.
Yarn Over after a purl and before a knit stitch—pass yarn over the top of right hand needle to back of work.

DUPLICATE STITCH—Fig. 17.

This covers knitted stitches with a contrasting color yarn, forming designs. Follow steps a, b, c, and d, being careful not to pull yarn too tight.

A

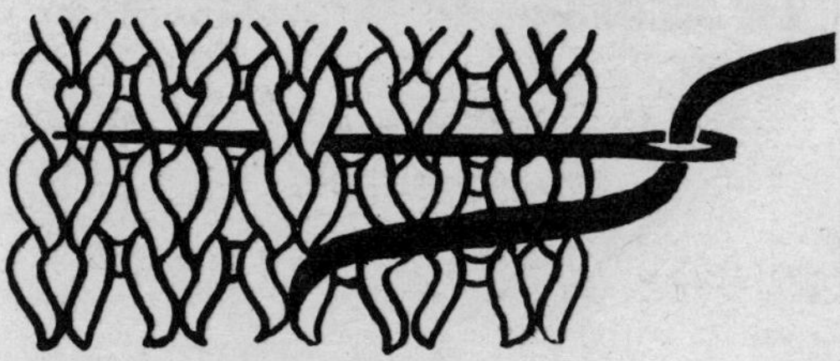

B

C

D

MULTICOLORED KNITTING—Fig. 18.

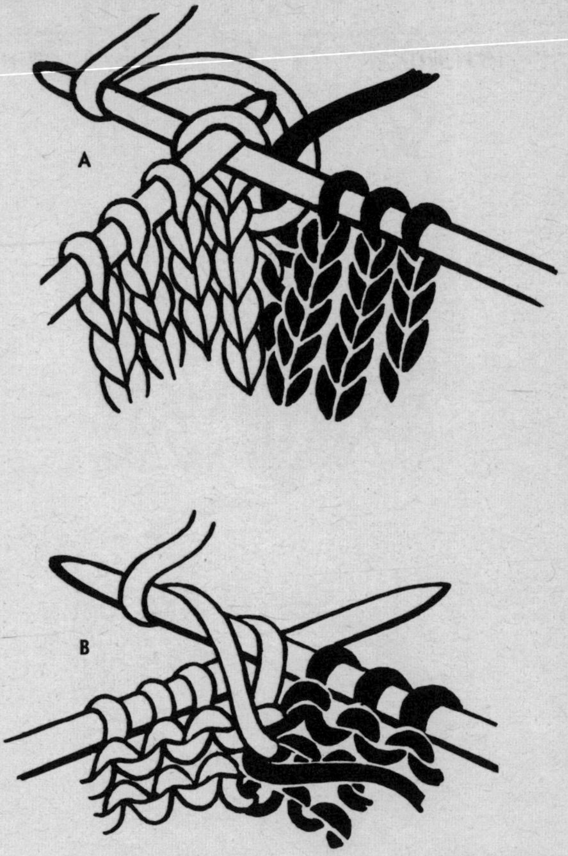

When changing colors, always bring the color to be used from under and around the color just dropped (a); this twists the yarns and avoids a hole in work. On the purl side of work twist yarns in the same manner (b). When carrying one color for more than 5 or 6 stitches, hold the unused color along the left hand needle and knit or purl under this strand, then on the next stitch drop the strand. This will secure strand against the row and will not show on right side of work. Carry unused color loosely across work on wrong side; to make sure it is loose enough, stretch out the stitches skipped to their widest extent on the right hand needle.

CABLE STITCH—Fig. 19.

Following directions of pattern, slip stitches to a cable stitch holder or double point needle and place in back of work, bring the yarn in front of these stitches then knit or purl the next stitches on the left hand needle as instructed; now work the stitches from the holder in their original order. When cable stitches are held in front of work, keep working strand in position in back.

Twisted or Crossed Stitches

TWISTED or CROSSED STITCHES

TWIST STITCH TO LEFT

With right-hand needle in back of left-hand needle, skip first stitch, knit into the back loop of 2nd stitch on left-hand needle and draw loop through (a), then knit or purl the skipped stitch as instructed (b). Slip both stitches from left-hand needle.

TWIST STITCH TO RIGHT

Skip first st on left-hand needle, insert right-hand needle in front loop of next stitch, yarn around needle and draw loop through (a), then knit or purl the skipped stitch as instructed (b). Slip both stitches from left-hand needle.

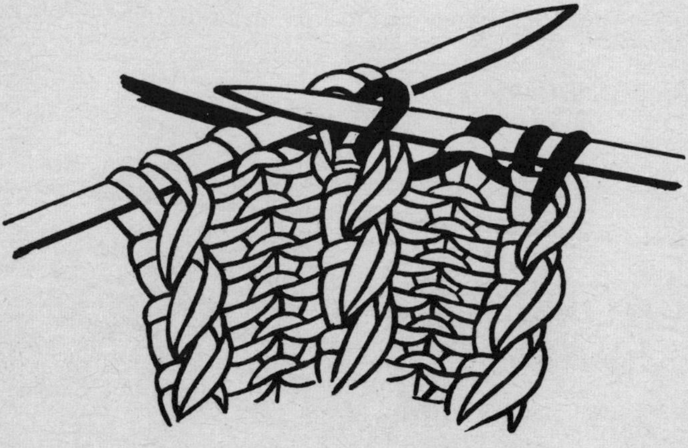

PICKING UP STITCHES—Fig. 20.

Hold work with right or wrong side to you as instructed, insert point of needle through at least 2 loops on the edge and pull yarn through, forming a stitch on right hand needle. For best results, insert needle into the knot or chain at end of rows. Directions tell how many stitches to pick up along a given space. To distribute picked up stitches evenly, divide the edge into halves or quarters, then pick up one-half or one-quarter of the total number in each section. It is often necessary to pick up a stitch between the end of rows to get the required amount of stitches. Along a cast-on or bound-off edge, pick up one stitch in each stitch.

BUTTONHOLES—Fig. 21.

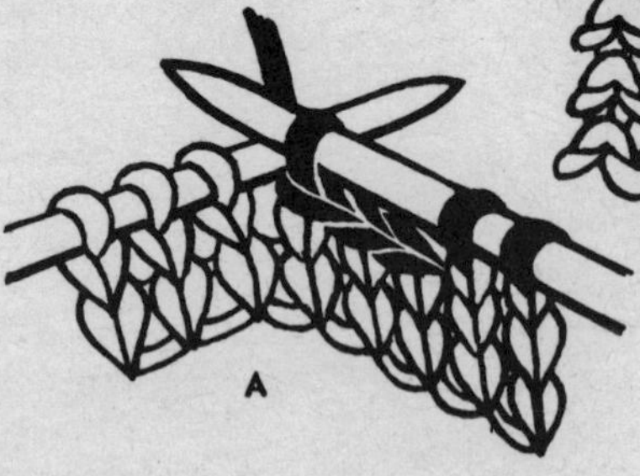

A

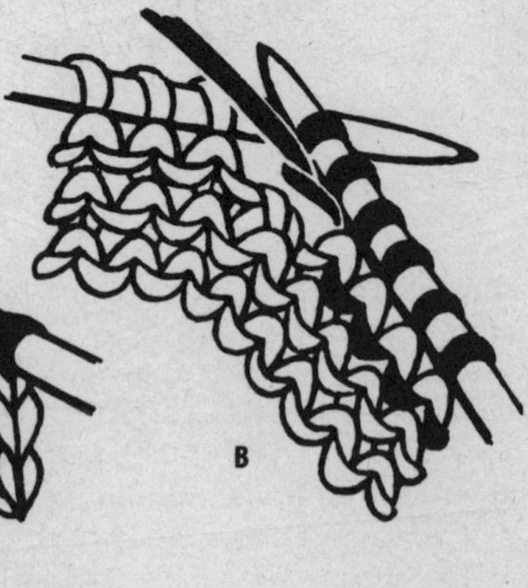

B

Two rows are necessary to make a buttonhole. Instructions usually read—"work x number of stitches, bind off next—stitches"—to do this, work x number of stitches then **work 2 more stitches** to start binding off; bind off the first of these 2 stitches, work another stitch, to bind off the next stitch as instructed; complete row. On the following row work to the opening, turn work to reverse side and cast on the required number of stitches using Second Method of Casting On. Turn work to right side and complete row. For very small buttonholes a "k 2 tog and yo" is frequently used. On the 2nd row the yo is worked as a stitch.

When finishing a garment overcast the buttonholes so that they are firm, using yarn or sewing thread.

Pocket Openings are frequently started in the same manner.

PICKING UP DROPPED STITCHES—Fig. 22.

It is easier to pick up stitches on the knit side of work. Insert a crochet hook into the loop of the dropped stitch * catch the loose strand of yarn of next row in back of the hook and pull loop through on hook. Repeat from * up each strand of yarn to needle. Stretch work a little widthwise so that each strand of yarn is in its proper sequence. Slip the last loop on the needle.

When picking up a dropped stitch in Garter stitch, it is necessary to reverse work each stitch, taking care to keep ridges even each row.

When necessary to take work off needles and rip back, rip to row before mistake. Rip one stitch at a time on next row inserting needle into each stitch from back to front as ripped. This places all stitches in correct position on needle.

SETTING IN SLEEVES—Fig. 23.

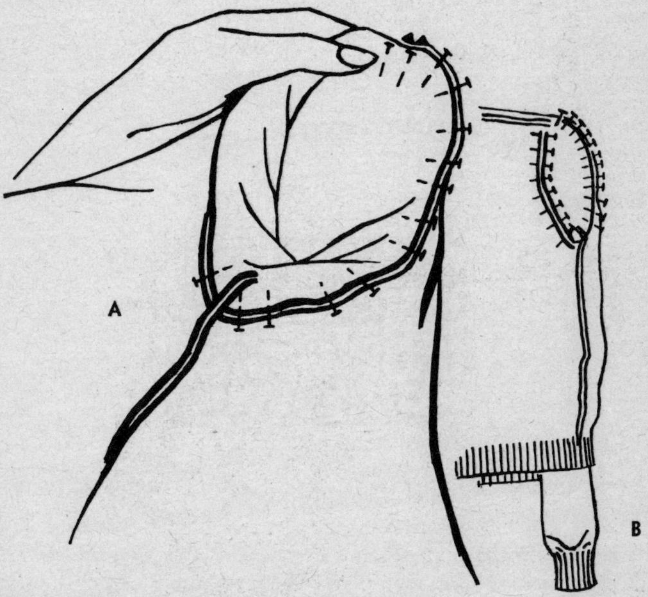

After seaming shoulders, pin center of cap of sleeve to shoulder seam, pin seam of sleeve to underarm seam (a). Pin all around easing in any fullness (b), taking care to match horizontal patterns and colors where necessary. Sew in sleeve using running and back stitches as explained in Fig. 24.

SEWING SEAMS—Fig. 24.

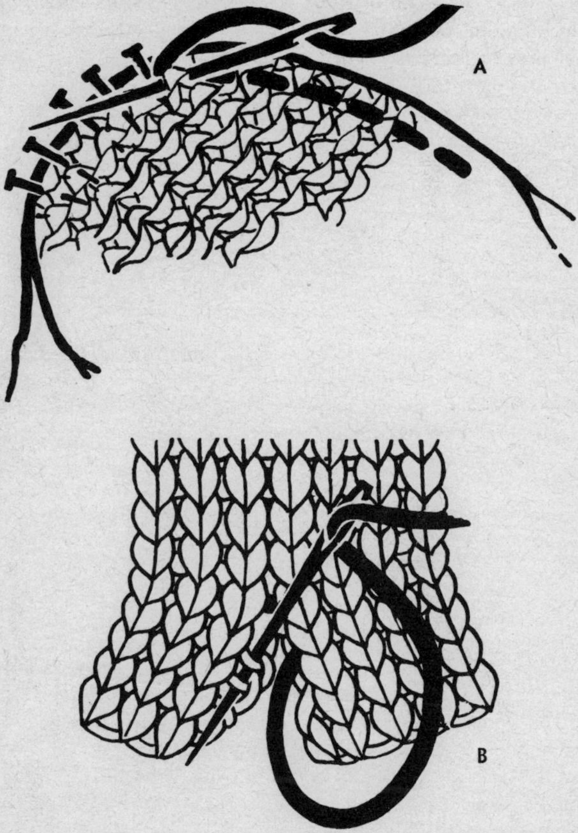

With right sides together, pin pieces evenly. Using a tapestry or wool (blunt point) needle, sew seams about ⅛ inch from edge, making 2 running stitches then one back stitch (a). When working with very heavy yarn, double thread can be used.

When sewing on right side of work (b), pin beginning and end of pieces to be seamed together. With right sides facing, insert needle between the first and second stitches from edge, working first on one piece then the other as pictured. About every one inch, work over same stitches twice to hold firmly. This method can be used along shoulders, matching bound off stitches of front and back.

TWISTED CORDS

Cut a strand of yarn about 5 times the length of desired finished cord and fold in half. Fasten one end securely to a drawer handle or knob to anchor. Twist doubled strand until it buckles. Holding end securely, place left hand in center of cord and right hand up against anchor, remove left hand and allow strand to twist on itself in the opposite direction. Remove from anchor, knot free ends together, cut off surplus. Smooth cord by pulling.

POMPONS

Pompon makers can be purchased and made from enclosed directions. Or, wind yarn around 2 fingers about 25-30 times; tie between fingers. Remove loops from fingers and again tie firmly in center, leaving about 8 inches for sewing. Clip loops, then trim to desired size.

Blocking

It is easier to block pieces before sewing them together. Where pieces are the same, such as sleeves, fronts or a back and front, block them together. With right sides facing, pin pieces together about 1 inch apart around all corresponding edges and lay on a flat padded surface. Take care that button and buttonhole bands are the same length. Pin pieces on surface to the measurements worked for length and width, having pins about 1 inch apart. If necessary to stretch pieces, spread from center to outer edges for an even distribution of stitches. Place a damp cloth (preferably dish towel type) over knitting and hold iron lightly on cloth allowing steam to form—do not rest the weight of the iron on the cloth. If a steam iron is used the cloth over the knitting should be dry. Steam entire surface on one side, then turn and steam the other piece in same manner. Allow to dry before sewing. Frequently it is advisable to again steam the seams after sewing. Do Not Press out ribbing unless so instructed.

Crochet Hooks

Crochet hooks are made of steel, aluminum and plastic.

Steel hooks range in size from 00 (largest size) to 15 (smallest size). Sizes used for yarns are from 00 to about sizes 3 or 4.

Aluminum and plastic hooks are in alphabetical order—A (smallest) to about J or K (largest). When sizes are given numerically for these hooks they range from 1 up, getting larger in size. This is the reverse of steel hooks. Care must be taken to use the appropriate size hook for each weight of yarn.

CHAIN (ch)—Fig. 25.

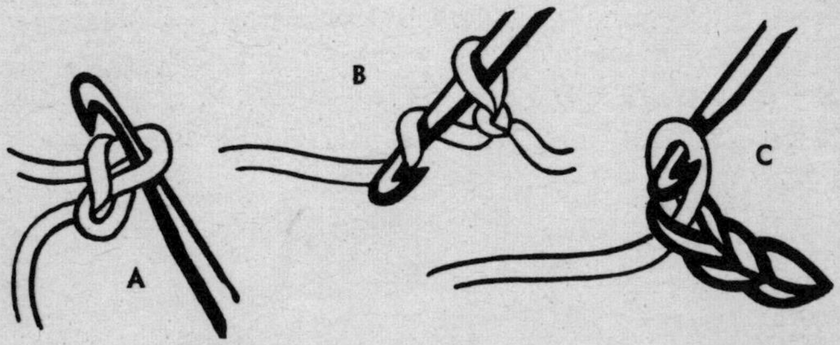

Make a slip loop at end of yarn, insert hook in the loop and pull to fit hook (a), * pass hook under and around yarn–this is called "thread over" or "yarn over" (b); draw hook up and yarn through loop on hook (c). This makes 1 chain stitch. Repeat from * as many times as directed.

SLIP STITCH (sl st)—Fig. 26.

A

B

When working on a chain, insert hook through 2nd chain from hook, * yarn over and draw through stitch (a) and through loop on hook (b), insert hook in next chain. Repeat from * as directed.

When working on an edge, hold yarn underneath garment, insert hook and draw yarn through to form first stitch, * insert hook in edge, draw yarn through edge and loop on hook. Repeat from * as directed.

SINGLE CROCHET (sc)—Fig. 27.

When working into a chain, insert hook in 2nd chain from hook, * yarn over and draw through stitch, yarn over and through both loops on hook, insert hook in next chain. Repeat from * as directed.

When working in previous row, * insert hook under the 2 top strands of stitch of row below, yarn over and draw through stitch (2 loops on hook), yarn over and through both loops on hook.

Repeat from * as directed. Occasionally instructions are given to work only into the back loop or front loop of row below.

HALF DOUBLE CROCHET (hdc)—Fig. 28.

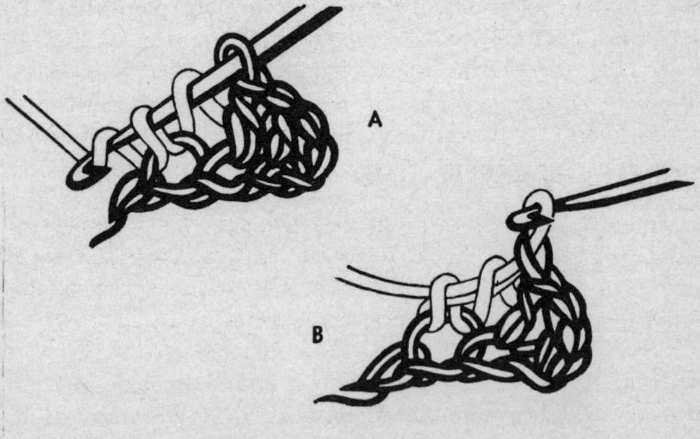

* Yarn over hook, insert hook under 2 top strands of stitch of row below, yarn over and draw through stitch (a), yarn over and through 3 loops on hook (b). Repeat from * as directed.

DOUBLE CROCHET (dc)—Fig. 29.

A

B

* Yarn over, insert hook in stitch, yarn over and through stitch—3 loops on hook (a), yarn over and draw through first 2 loops on hook—2 loops remain on hook—(b), yarn over and draw through remaining 2 loops. Repeat from * as directed.

SINGLE CROCHET EDGING

* Insert hook in stitch and pull loop through, yarn over and draw through both loops on hook. Repeat from * as directed. Care must be taken so that the edge will lie flat. To determine the number of stitches for a flat edge, make a chain, work single crochet in 2nd chain from hook and each chain. Now measure the gauge (number of stitches per inch). Mark off edge of garment into 2-inch spaces and make the correct number of crocheted stitches in each 2 inches of edge.

A double strand of yarn worked into a crocheted chain can be used as ties for bonnets or laced through beading rows wherever cords are needed.

ABBREVIATIONS

beg	beginning	psso	pass slip st over
dec(s)	decrease(s)–(ing)	p	purl
dp	double point	rnd(s)	round(s)
inc(s)	increase(s)–(ing)	sl	slip
lp(s)	loop(s)	st(s)	stitch(es)
k	knit	tog	together
pat(s)	pattern(s)	yo	yarn over needle

* **(asterisk)** . . . follow the directions from the * as many times as specified in addition to the original wording.

** **(double asterisk)** . . . are used in the same manner as single asterisks in a different part of a row or round.

( ) **parentheses in a row** . . . work the stitches between the ( )'s as many times as specified, for example–(K 2 tog, k 1) 3 times is the same as–k 2 tog, k 1, k 2 tog, k 1, k 2 tog, k 1.

CROCHET ABBREVIATIONS

ch	chain	hdc	half double crochet
sc	single crochet	tr c	treble crochet
dc	double crochet	sl st	slip stitch

MARKERS

To Place a Marker on Needles—slip a small plastic ring on needle, or make a loop of yarn to replace ring. Slip marker on every row or round until you are told to remove it.

To Mark One Row—tie a bit of contrasting color yarn or thread to center of row or at end of row if so directed.

To Mark Rows for Counting—use a length of contrasting color yarn about 18 inches long. After 10 rows have been worked, insert yarn between two stitches about 1 inch from edge when working next row. Work 10 more rows (these are easier to count on the purl side), bring one end of yarn forward between the same two stitches. Continue to weave the strand back and forth alternately every 10th row. Rows can be marked in the same way for increases and decreases by weaving the strand between two stitches on every increase or decrease row.

Work Even . . . Work in pattern on stitches as set up without increasing or decreasing.

EQUIVALENT AMERICAN AND BRITISH KNITTING NEEDLES

American	0	1	2	3	4	5	6
British	13	12	11	10	9	8	7
American	7	8	9	10	10½	13	15
British	6	5	4	3	2	1	000

FRENCH ABBREVIATIONS

k	point endroit
p	point envers
st(s)	point(s)
beg	commencement
dec(s)	diminuez—diminutions
inc(s)	augmentez—augmentations
tog	ensemble
pat(s)	points fantasie
yo	jeté
psso	passer point glissé
lp(s)	boucle(s)
sl	glisser
dp	d'aiguilles
rnd(s)	rang
ch	chainette
sc	maille serrée
hdc	demi-bride
dc	bride
slip st	point glissé
work even	travaillez
* (signe de répétition)	suivez les instructions de * jusqu'au mot "répétez"; ensuite recommencez à * autant de fois qu'indiqué *en plus* des instructions premières.

These French words and phrases have been supplied by needlework experts in their native language. Several linguists have checked and found them accurate and helpful for the directions in this book.

GERMAN ABBREVIATIONS

k	rechts stricken
p	links stricken
st(s)	masche(n)
beg	anfang oder anschlag
dec(s)	abnehmen
inc(s)	aufnehmen
tog	zusammen
pat(s)	mustersatz
yo	umschlag
psso	die abgehobene Masche ueberziehen
lp(s)	schlinge(n)
sl	schlüpfen
dp	hilssnadeln
rnd(s)	runde(n)
ch	luftmasche(n)
sc	feste masche(n)
hdc	halbstaebchen
dc	staebchen
work even	gerade arbeiten ohne auf–oder abnehmen
* (stern)	von * bis zum Wort wiederholen weiterarbeiten, dann beginne vom * sovielmal wie zum Original-wortsatz zusaetzlich angegeben.

These German words and phrases have been supplied by needlework experts in their native language. Several linguists have checked and found them accurate and helpful for the directions in this book.

ITALIAN ABBREVIATIONS

k	maglia—diritto
p	rovescio
st(s)	punto
beg	principio—cominciare
dec(s)	calatura—diminuire
inc(s)	aumentare
tog	insieme
pat(s)	motivo—disegno
yo	filo sopra il ferro
psso	fare 1 punto poi passarlo sopra quello che segue
lp(s)	punto lungo sciolto o cappio
dp	doppio punto
rnd(s)	giro—giri
sl	passare o scivolare
ch	catena
sc	crochet
hdc	mezzo doppio crochet
dc	doppio crochet
work even	seguire il disegno senza aumentare ne diminuire
* (asterisco)	seguire la direzione da * poi ripetere, dopo cominciare da tante volte quanto è indicato sull' istruzione del lavoro.

These Italian words and phrases have been supplied by needlework experts in their native language. Several linguists have checked and found them accurate and helpful for the directions in this book.

SPANISH ABBREVIATIONS

k	derecho
p	reves
st(s)	puntada(s)
beg	comenzar
dec(s)	disminuir—disminuyendo
inc(s)	aumentar—aumentando
tog	junto
pat(s)	patron(es)
yo	hilo sobre la aguja
psso	dejar pasar una puntada
lp(s)	gacita(s)
sl	pasar sin trabajando
dp	punto doble
rnd(s)	redondo(s) ó vuelta
ch	cadeneta
sc	crochet sencillo
hdc	mitad de doble crochet
dc	crochet doble
work even	trabajar sin aumentar ni disminuir
* (asteriscos)	siga las instrucciónes desde el * hasta la palabra repetida, entonces empezar desde el * tantas veces como sean especificadas en adición a las explicaciónes ó instrucciónes originales.

These Spanish words and phrases have been supplied by needlework experts in their native language. Several linguists have checked and found them accurate and helpful for the directions in this book.

3 PLY FINGERING YARNS

Here is a chart of yarns that can be worked to the same gauge as the types recommended in this book.

MANUFACTURERS	3 Ply Fingering Yarn 100% wool	3 Ply Nylon & Wool 50/50	Nylon Fingering Yarn
AMERICAN THREAD COMPANY	"Dawn" DeLuxe Fingering		"Dawn" Nylon, 3 Ply
BEAR BRAND FLEISHER YARNS	Ever Match Sock & Fingering, 3 Ply or DeLuxe Sock & Sport, 3 Ply	Nylon 'n Wool	Super Spun Nylon
BERNAT	Jaeger Classic Fingering, 3 Ply	Meadowspun 50/50	Nylon
COATS & CLARK	"Red Heart" Super Fingering, 3 Ply	"Red Heart" Nylon and Wool, 3 Ply	"Red Heart" Nylon, 3 ply
COLUMBIA-MINERVA	Beehive Scotch Fingering and Columbia-Minerva Fingering	Nylon & Wool Fingering	
S. S. KRESGE CO.		Green Oak Nylon & Wool Fingering	
GOLD BELL	Sport 'n' Finger-ing, 3 Ply		Nylon
MAJESTY	Sport 'n' Finger-ing, 3 Ply		Nylon
J.C. PENNEY		"Good Shepherd" Fingering Yarn Nylon & Wool 50/50	Penney's Nylon Yarn, 100% CrimpSet.
SPINNERIN	Candour	Nylaine Fingering Yarn	

SPORTS YARNS

Here is a chart of yarns that can be worked to the same gauge as the types recommended in this book.

MANUFACTURERS	Sports Yarn 100% Wool	Sports Yarn Nylon & Wool 50/50	Sayelle Nantuk or Orlon Sayelle of Sports Yarn Weight
AMERICAN THREAD COMPANY			"Dawn" Orlon, 3 Ply
BEAR BRAND FLEISHER YARNS	Casa-Laine Sport Yarn; Ever Match Sport and Sweater Yarn; Spice	Ever Match Germantown Sport, Nylon 'n Wool	
BERNAT	Sportsyarn	Nylo Sports 50/50	
COATS & CLARK		"Red Heart" Nylon & Wool Sport Yarn	
COLUMBIA-MINERVA	Princessa Sports or Feather-weight Knitting Worsted	Skylark Quick Knitting Sports Yarn; Alpaca & Nylon Sports Yarn	Nantuk Sports Yarn
S. S. KRESGE CO.	Green Oak Sport Yarn		
J.C. PENNEY		Penney's Germantown Sports 50/50	
REYNOLDS	Versailles		
SPINNERIN		Nylaine Germantown Sport Yarn	Orlon Sayelle Sport Yarn

KNITTING WORSTED WEIGHT YARNS

Here is a chart of yarns that can be worked to the same gauge as the types recommended in this book.

MANUFACTURERS	Knitting Worsted	Nylon & Wool of Knitting Worsted Weight	Machine Washable Sayelle Nantuk or Orlon of Knitting Worsted Weight
AMERICAN THREAD COMPANY	"Dawn" Knitting Worsted		"Dawn" Sayelle Knitting Worsted
BEAR BRAND FLEISHER YARNS	Knitting Worsted	Jiffy Nylon 'n Wool Knitting Worsted	Orlon Sayelle, 4 Ply Orlon Wintuk
BERNAT	Super Knitting Worsted or Knitting Worsted	Nylo Germantown or Nylo Knitting Worsted	
COATS & CLARK	"Red Heart" Knitting Worsted		"Red Heart" Sayelle
COLUMBIA-MINERVA	Knitting Worsted	Calypso	Nantuk Knitting Worsted
GOLD BELL	Knitting Worsted		Orlon Sayelle Knitting Worsted Weight
S. S. KRESGE CO.	Green Oak Knitting Worsted		Green Oak Orlon and Orlon Sayelle
MAJESTY	Knitting Worsted		Orlon Sayell Knitting Worsted Weight
J.C. PENNEY	Penney's Knitting Worsted	Penney's Germantown Knitting Worsted 50/50	Penney's Orlon Sayelle or Nantuk Knitting Worsted Type
SPINNERIN	Marvel Twist	Nylaine Germantown Knitting Worsted	Orlon Sayelle Express; Nantuk or Wintuk Knitting Worsted

BULKY YARNS

Here is a chart of yarns that can be worked to the same gauge as the types recommended in this book.

MANUFACTURERS	Quick Knit Bulky Yarns 100% Wool	Quick Knit Bulky Nylon & Wool 50/50	EXTRA BULKY YARNS
AMERICAN THREAD COMPANY		"Dawn" Bulky Nylon & Wool	
BEAR BRAND FLEISHER YARNS	Bulky Knit	Bulky Knit Nylon & Wool 50/50	Nubby Fleece Big Spice Gigantic
BERNAT			Shakerspun
COATS & CLARK		"Red Heart" Turbo-Knit	
COLUMBIA-MINERVA	Calibar Bulky Nantuk	Calibrette	Contempo
GOLD BELL		Bulky Yarn	
S. S. KRESGE CO.		Green Oak Bulky Knit Yarn	
MAJESTY		Bulky Yarn	
J.C. PENNEY		Penney's Bulky Knit Yarn 50/50	Penney's Shakerspun
SPINNERIN	Ski Sprint	Nylaine Quick Knit	Homespun

MOHAIR AND MOHAIR BLENDED YARNS

Care must be taken when buying Mohair yarns to distinguish between 40-gram and 1-ounce balls. 28 grams equal 1 ounce, therefore a 40-gram ball is just under 1½ ounces.

In the first column are listed 100% Mohair and Mohair Blended Yarns of a uniform size that will work to the gauge given in the directions for the individual garment. This category is the heavier of the two types used in this book.

In the second column are again 100% Mohair and Mohair Blended Yarns of a uniform and lighter-weight size that will work to the gauge given in the directions for individual garments.

MANUFACTURERS	Mohair & Mohair Blends Heavier Weight	Mohair & Mohair Blends Light Weight
BEAR BRAND FLEISHER YARNS	Supra Mohair 100% Bucilla Mohara Bucilla Mist-Aire	
BERNAT	Mohairspun Mohair Plus Molaine	
COATS & CLARK	"Red Heart" Mohcora	
COLUMBIA-MINERVA	Roma	Reverie
S. S. KRESGE CO.		Green Oak Mohair Blend 70/30
J.C. PENNEY	Contessa 100%	
REYNOLDS	Super Cabri	Mohair No. 1. 100%
SPINNERIN	Cortina 100% Mohair 1001	Frostlon Petite